Praise for *The Perfect Ofsted Inspection*

A highly practical and comprehensive guide that will ensure that you show your school and its achievements at its best. *The Perfect Ofsted Inspection* skilfully provides advice and guidance alongside actual case studies of how the advice works in practice. This book is a must for any leadership team, middle leader and governing body. Read in conjunction with *The Perfect Ofsted Lesson*, all schools should be better placed to meet the demands of the Ofsted visit.

Julie Summerfield, Head Teacher,
Horndean Technology College

The Perfect Ofsted Inspection offers school leaders a cogent and concise analysis of the challenges of the new Ofsted framework. In addition it offers school leaders comprehensive and competent solutions to ensure that the 'outstanding' judgement is lived, breathed and witnessed in the daily life of the school.

As with her previous books, Jackie has once again developed her own outstanding practice of separating the kernels from the husks and allowing the school leader to plan, prepare and prioritise strategies for school improvement in order to reach the 'promised land' of 'outstanding'.

Her style remains witty and her anecdotes informative, and such a personalised style adds to the enjoyment of a subject matter that can sometimes appear rather stale on the surface. She brings to life the importance of ensuring that schools are places where staff and students ought to progress daily. In this way, as a school leader, I found the book not only to be informative but also transformative.

John Toal, Director of Ethos,
Learning and Teaching, St Ambrose College

Jackie Beere's book *The Perfect Ofsted Inspection* is an essential guide to preparing for the 2012 inspection framework. It covers everything from self-evaluation to using Parent View effectively, from pointers for governors and teaching assistants to teachers and the senior leadership team. It is succinctly written with good real-life examples of outstanding practice. It is an effective summary of what a school should have in place to achieve the best Ofsted possible and it is accessible for all involved in school improvement.

We all live with the shadow of Ofsted and Jackie's book provides some bright lights to help diminish this shadow. *The Perfect Ofsted Inspection* gives schools the confidence to strive to be outstanding, to be open with inspectors and clear in the process of the inspection.

Mark Ratchford, Head Teacher,
Glapthorn CE Lower School, Northamptonshire

The Perfect Ofsted Inspection is more than a useful addition to the literature – it is essential reading. It is also easy to like. I read it in two sessions and will read it again with a pen in hand to create a to-do list.

The book is very readable on account of the lively style, well-chosen case studies, checklists and summaries. It stands in stark contrast to the worthy tomes we all buy and never have the heart to read.

The author is suitably authoritative and brisk – and understands that a bit of bossiness saves busy staff a lot of time. Buy it.

Tim Bartlett, former head teacher

THE PERFECT INSPECTION

Ofsted

Jackie Beere Edited by Ian Gilbert

 Independent Thinking Press

First published by

Independent Thinking Press
Crown Buildings, Bancyfelin, Carmarthen, Wales, SA33 5ND, UK
www.independentthinkingpress.com

Independent Thinking Press is an imprint of Crown House Publishing Ltd.

British Library Cataloguing-in-Publication Data
A catalogue entry for this book is available
from the British Library.

Print ISBN 978-1-78135-000-3
Mobi ISBN 978-1-78135-021-8
ePub ISBN 978-1-78135-022-5

Printed and bound in the UK by
Gomer Press, Llandysul, Ceredigion

Dedicated to my perfect mum and dad!

Contents

Acknowledgements

One of the greatest pleasures of my latest career as a school improvement partner, author, consultant and trainer has been to work with inspirational head teachers and other school leaders who are dedicated to creating amazing opportunities for the learners in their schools. This book is dedicated to those who are brave enough to take on the top job, with all the challenges and opportunities it presents.

On the roller coaster of school leadership there is little more rewarding than being judged by other professionals as 'outstanding' – and the benefits to your school that follow are very well known. I wanted to try to capture some of the most inspiring practice I have seen in this book, so other teachers and leaders can have the very best chance to impress.

Many thanks go to my case study schools for sharing their wonderful work with me. Thank you in particular to Ranjit Samra, Colin Turner and Martin Moore. The years I have worked alongside you have been a great pleasure and an inspiring learning journey.

I would like to thank Gulshan Kayembe for generously sharing her Ofsted expertise and taking time to give me such

Acknowledgments

useful feedback. She made me believe we can all work together to make the inspection process work for our schools. This book would not have happened if not for the encouragement of Caroline Lenton and support from Ian Gilbert and everyone else at Crown House/Independent Thinking Press, who are the most lovely bunch of publishing people you could meet.

Thank you also to my daughters, Carrie for the initial 'Perfect' inspiration, and to Lucy for constantly keeping me in touch with the life of a teacher in the classroom – I am so very proud of how resilient and determined you both are – in everything.

Finally, I must acknowledge my husband John. He made this book work so much better through his incessant attention to detail and talent for organising my often chaotic prose into something that makes sense. He is the other half of my brain, as well as my rock and my greatest supporter.

What a wonderful thing it is to write books that someone wants to read – books that may help a bit with the hugely important job of leading and teaching in schools. How lucky am I to be able to do this job! If you are reading this – thanks …

Foreword

Clint Eastwood rides into town and goes into the saloon. He's been told the whole place needs a good shake-up. Several minutes later he leaves, guns smoking, and rides off into the sunset leaving behind a bar where the staff who haven't been sacked or shot are demoralised and wondering why they ever went into the saloon-keeping business in the first place.

Down the road, a professional and committed lady bar owner is taking her staff through what they need to do to be even better at their job. She is firm but human, making her best bar staff feel great about what they do yet want to be even better, and helping those who are less good raise their game. Throughout the process she keeps the whole staff focused on core bar-keeping principles that remind everyone why working in a saloon is the best job in the whole world.

And so, in a (not too far-fetched metaphor of a) nutshell, there you have the state of school inspection in the UK today.

On the one hand you have a gung-ho approach driven by the 'fact' that if you scratch the surface of any teacher you will find a complacent slacker who needs his arse kicked in order to do a half-decent job for those poor children not lucky enough to get an independent education. On the other, you have people like Jackie Beere who has spent her life in schools at all levels of the system, who is one of the UK's most respected and innovative educational pioneers and who knows that education is not about (although does involve) grades and league tables. Instead improving education is about helping teachers plan lessons that genuinely engage learners in the process of learning as well as developing skills and competencies that will help them thrive in the twenty-first century workplace.

Which is where this book comes in.

Building on the phenomenal success of her *Perfect Ofsted Lesson* book for the Independent Thinking Press, *The Perfect Ofsted Inspection* takes the reader simply but assertively through all that any school needs to do in order to present themselves in the best possible light next time Clint and his team of gunslingers ride into town.

But this is not a book about simply doing well in an Ofsted inspection. Jackie's own brand of school improvement runs far deeper than mere window dressing. What's more, surprising though it may seem at first glance, the new Ofsted framework and Jackie's passion for genuine quality in educational experience do converge nicely. Developing independent learning, moving away – well away – from an over-reliance on 'chalk and talk' lessons, providing opportunities for developing skills and competencies, genuinely engaging learners in their own learning, planning for and measuring progress, using assessment and data as tools to support learning, working at an emotional as well as an intellectual level – all of these have been staples in Jackie's work for many years. Nice now of Ofsted to catch up.

Quality teaching and learning in the classroom on its own does not an 'outstanding school' make however. Schools still regularly let themselves down at leadership level. This is why Jackie's new book behaves like the love child of an authoritative guide and an expert coach standing there with a simple checklist and a firm but caring face to ensure that all school leaders – from the head and governors to the heads of department and middle leaders – get the basics right. Basics that are relevant whatever type of school you are and whether you are about to be on the receiving end of a visit from Clint or not.

Education is a political football and it is a political game as old as the hills to decry something publicly in order to achieve the leverage with the public and the press to make significant (often self-serving and ideological) changes. It's the same with the National Health Service. To ride into town all guns blazing under a banner of 'making things better' is cheap, easy leadership, whether you are the Secretary of State for Education, the head of Ofsted, the executive director an academy chain or a head teacher. To walk purposefully into town with a genuine desire to introduce lasting improvements firmly and professionally that bring the best out of all hard-working and committed staff is something that takes a much greater degree of professionalism and skill. We are all fortunate that Jackie Beere is able to show us this alternative approach to improvement before all the saloon keepers give up, pack up and head for the hills.

Ian Gilbert
Santiago
Valentine's Day 2012

Introduction

An Ofsted inspection is *the* key performance indicator. Every school wants to get it right because the consequences are huge for the head, the staff, the students and the whole community. Getting it right means ensuring that the judgements made are fair and justified. Unfortunately, there are schools that feel the judgements Ofsted have made got their school wrong.

This book has been written to help you to make sure that your school does all that it can to ensure that the judgements are not only right, but 'good' or 'outstanding'. If you follow the advice given here you'll be able to embed great learning and leadership that is sustainable and which will continue to deliver the very best results for your pupils.

Working over the years as an advanced skills teacher, head, school improvement partner, consultant and trainer in so many schools, I have seen the very best and the very worst practice. I have also seen excellent schools that have not been able to show off their strengths, leading to judgements that have been wrong (and vice versa). With a new evaluation schedule, framework and head of Ofsted in 2012, now is the perfect time to consider how to prepare your school be the best it can be.

2012

The 2012 inspection framework intends to focus only on areas that have the most impact on improving educational outcomes, making judgements in just four areas:

- The achievement of pupils in the school
- The quality of teaching in the school
- The behaviour and safety of pupils at the school
- The quality of leadership and management in the school

At the same time inspectors will look at how well the school meets the needs of *all* pupils (see Chapter 2) and how it promotes their spiritual, moral, social and cultural development to also make a judgement on:

- The overall effectiveness of the school

The triangulation of attainment data, classroom practice and leadership priorities will still define the quality of the leadership and the provision of the school. The key is to ensure that all of the above bullet points are fully addressed and equally 'outstanding'.

In making their judgements, inspectors *must* consider which descriptor best fits the evidence available. When evidence indicates that *any* of the bullet points in the descriptor for inadequate applies, then that aspect of the school's work *should* be judged inadequate.

Ofsted, *Evaluation Schedule for the Inspection of Maintained Schools and Academies* (2012): 5

So what else is in the new framework?

- More observation of teaching
- A stronger focus on behaviour for learning
- A focus on embedded Assessment for Learning as a high priority
- The expectation that there is rigorous performance management which deals with underperformance effectively. The inspection team will be using observations of teaching and learning to judge how effective the leadership is in improving teaching and learning. This includes addressing 'inadequate' teaching but now also raising 'satisfactory' teaching to 'good' and 'good' to 'outstanding'
- An expectation that every lesson will have evidence of planning to close the achievement gap, with a special focus on underperforming groups of students

- A new and demanding emphasis on judging standards of oracy, literacy and numeracy in primary schools, and oracy and literacy in *all* subjects in secondary schools
- Scrutiny of policy and practice for engaging with parents that has a positive impact on closing the achievement gap for those children most in need

Sounds daunting? It could be if you're not prepared – especially with only two days' notice. With the latest news now suggesting that by September 2012 all schools could be subject to 'no notice' inspections, there is even more reason to install and embed the very best practice.

The aim for all of us is to have a school that we are proud for anyone to inspect – any time, any day – because we know that what we do each day, each week, each year is to offer students great learning. Nothing is 'perfect'. This book aims to help you embed best practice over a period of time – not just for the sake of an inspection but to ensure the very best outcomes for your pupils at *all* times.

Chapter 1
Embedding your vision

Becoming an 'outstanding' school is not quick or easy. In fact, it is the result of relentless hard work and determination over time. The 2012 framework and evaluation schedule are not trying to make it harder but are focusing more on what really matters – how well individual pupils benefit from their school. This depends on the senior leadership team (SLT) putting in place the long-term strategies which encourage outstanding lessons and hence, outstanding outcomes. This chapter deals with these strategies while Chapter 2 focuses on the elements of outstanding lessons.

'Outstanding' schools have employed the following long-term strategies:

- Growing the vision and culture with everyone
- Embedding the habits that will make the difference
- Embedding the seven habits of highly effective teachers – and pupils
- Getting middle leaders to buy in

- Ensuring effective performance management and continuous professional development
- Engaging with the whole school community
- Rigorous self-evaluation – know thyself!
- Using the self-evaluation form to produce a live school development plan

Strategy 1. Growing the vision and culture with everyone

What is your school famous for? What is your head's vision for the school? What are the key priorities for improvement? Which are the underperforming groups and what is being done about them?

Everyone in your school needs to know the answers to these questions – the students, parents, admin staff, teachers, student teachers, governors and so on. No matter that the vision is expressed in a slogan on the school badge, no matter how many times you have repeated it, the vision isn't embedded until it runs through the school like the lettering in a stick of rock. This means wherever you look you see the vision – writ large everywhere. It is on the displays, in the pupils' behaviour, in the staffroom and voiced by the governors. The reception desk, the corridors, the furniture and, above all, the atmosphere in every classroom needs to reek of your school vision, so that when the Ofsted team enters the school, they get a whiff!

Every school has similar aspirations in their vision – so what is special about yours? It is important that it reflects your particular community and its distinct needs and desires and is set in the context of our complex, connected world. It sounds simple but this vision will be what drives you forward in all your strategic decisions, training events, development planning and staffing priorities – and it should do. If your school lives and breathes the vision this will permeate general staffroom conversation and underpin and act as a focus for staff-driven initiatives.

'I can't wait for the SLT to come to my lesson so I can show off my latest risk-taking, creative plenary and show how the students turn hideous mistakes into exciting learning experiences.'

Staffroom conversations say so much about a school. But in schools I've visited that were deemed 'outstanding' there was a pervasive sense of shared culture and professional reflective practice. There is a sense of community, a love of the job, wanting people to see your lessons, feeling valued and able to take risks and truly believing you can – and are – having a powerful impact on outcomes. This is the ethos that has to be encouraged by the head teacher and the SLT.

Growing that vision and culture together is a long-term project and therefore needs time to seed, be nurtured and take root across the whole school community. The leadership team will need to be relentless in weeding out the distractions, deviations, detractors and doubters during this delicate growth period. They need to keep the faith until the benefits begin to be felt in terms of positive outcomes and well-being that will result from everyone really pulling in the same direction and sharing the same values.

Summary

- Check out your vision for the school – is it still relevant to local needs?
- Is it ambitious and aspirational (and concise)?
- Do the staff own it, know it and believe in it?
- Do the students?
- Does your most cynical member of staff value it?
- Walk down the corridor – can you see it in practice everywhere?
- Does the SLT walk the talk too?
- Does it drive everything you do?
- Is it habitual?

[Inspectors should focus on] how relentlessly leaders, managers and the governing body pursue a vision for excellence, for example through ... the extent to which staff, pupils, parents and carers are engaged by and contribute to realising the vision and ambition of the leaders, managers and governors.

Ofsted, *Evaluation Schedule for the Inspection of Maintained Schools and Academies* (2012): 18

'You know you've cracked it when a visitor remarks to a student, "Everyone here is very polite in corridors" and the student says, "Oh do you think so, I haven't really noticed. It's just the way we are here."'

Strategy 2. Embedding the habits that will make the difference

When the vision has grown across the school and is fully established, then unconscious, positive habits shown by staff and pupils will constantly demonstrate its pervasive influence on the culture of the school. These positive habitual behaviours are what the Ofsted team are looking out for when they wander the school watching staff and talking to pupils.

Bad habits are hard to break because they work at a subconscious level and are extremely contagious. What are the habits at your school? Do staff:

- Tend to stay late or leave early?
- Moan about the students or about the leadership?
- Boast about the school's achievements down the pub?
- Put a positive slant on the results at the end of the year?
- Leave their classroom doors open?
- Share ideas for developing independent learning across departments?

Do some departments have their own individual mini-culture? Is it built around a leader who supports or undermines the whole school direction? We all recognise staffroom chat about say, the science department – how they always do their own thing and don't buy into our 'creative curriculum'. (See Strategy 4 below for the vital importance of all middle leaders being part of the culture you need to develop.) Consistency of ethos across the whole school is the key to sustainability, so getting everyone to buy in to your message and implementing it relentlessly – and habitually – in their own classroom is essential.

Developing and embedding the habits that will sustain and feed your vision is an important part of your long-term preparation for Ofsted. The thinking behind a 'drop-in' inspection for 'satisfactory' schools is to ensure that good practice is embedded and habitual, and not a show or a performance for two days. The focus of the follow-up visit will be to see how well the school is implementing the areas identified for improvement.

The advantage of embedding best practice, of course, is that it can only be good for learning, for students and for results. So what are those vital habits we need to embed and how do we do it?

First we have to recognise the bad habits and then want to change them because we believe in the new behaviours. Next we have to practise them over and over again without defaulting back to old habits (which die hard!).

A good example is Assessment for Learning. No school (apart from some in the independent sector) has missed out on the training for AfL. The need to set objectives and targets, use peer- and self-assessment, have thinking time, plenaries and so on has been on the INSET agenda for several years. Yet Ofsted finds that this good practice, which we know will work, has not properly embedded. Teachers do not habitually use it to inform their planning for progress in learning.

For many teachers, the scheme of work drives their delivery. They are not sensitive enough to when and how the learners learn. Teachers may plan three-part lessons and try to use a variety of methods, apart from teacher talk, to engage learn-ers. But have they really bought into the habit of rigorous monitoring of the progress children are making? Is setting objectives merely a routine 'Write your objective down in your book'? Is there always a meaningful dialogue in classrooms about what the learning is to be and then about how effective it has been? Are most lessons routinely teacher-led? Do observed lessons reflect the norm? Ask your staff (and students) for an honest answer ...

So what habits do we want to see and how do we nurture the best ones? Some habits will naturally arise from the vision. For example:

'Our vision is learning without limits'

Habitual behaviours for staff and students: a belief that intelligence is learnable and every child can achieve; very high expectations for all students evident in every lesson seen and in every wall display, arts production, pastoral charity ambition, special educational needs support service, etc.; teachers involved in action research and delivering their own continuing professional development (CPD).

'Our vision is for strong community and collaboration'

Habitual behaviours for staff and students: a belief in personal development and employability skills alongside high academic expectations; outstanding development of group work underpinned by vertical tutor groups and cross-phase, cross-curricular learning; departments working together, team teaching and electronic sharing of resources; members of the community used regularly as part of teaching teams.

'Our vision is for academic excellence'

Habitual behaviours for staff and students: a belief in a traditional academic curriculum and powerful knowledge base; celebration of academic success and subject expertise through clubs and specialisms; intellectual debate and discussion with healthy competition between subjects; valuing of subject expertise and ability streaming to gain the best results.

Top tips

Here are some suggestions from Alan Brookes, head teacher at Fulston Manor School, a large 11–18 non-selective school in a selective authority in Kent, which was inspected under the 2012 pilot and received an 'outstanding' in all four categories:

- Create a culture from which achievement can grow
- The physical environment is crucial – old buildings and mobiles can be clean and free of graffiti and litter
- Nobody learns (or teaches well) if they are unhappy
- There is no contradiction between order and discipline and a belief that being at school should be full of laughter and joy
- 'Everybody matters, everybody succeeds, everybody helps' – judgements are made on the cohesion of the whole community of teachers and learners

- Ofsted success is based on replicating during inspection the good practice that occurs all the time, not on attempting to introduce last minute change
- Create a system that links CPD to individual classroom performance and personal need as well as whole school priorities
- Recruit, develop and promote outstanding staff and let them get on with it
- Be informed and accountable for every child and every member of staff
- Burn with passion, enthusiasm, aspiration and relentless optimism – and ensure the inspectors feel the heat

From the head's regular blog on the school's website:

I know that at the core of it all is my belief that success arises from the culture of a school, from the happiness of students and staff. Success is about changing children's lives, modelling and acting out the civilised values and codes by which we would like everybody to live. It's about joy and astonishment and excitement and risk and enterprise and adventure. Of course qualifications are important in improving children's life chances but they should grow naturally from everything else that is occurring ... This is the engine which powers Fulston Manor and makes it the school that it is.

And from the school's Ofsted report:

Fulston Manor is an outstanding school. The strong leadership of the head teacher, allied to the support offered from an excellent and dedicated staff, has ensured that the school has built successfully on its previously identified strengths and has continued to improve at an impressive rate. This improvement has been helped by the accuracy of the school's self-evaluation. This has ensured that areas where performance has been less effective have been addressed. Partnerships with other schools in the vicinity have benefited the students, especially in the sixth form, through offering access to a broad and highly relevant curriculum. Key Stages 3 and 4 students have benefited from many different curriculum initiatives associated with the school's business and enterprise status. Encouraging students to adopt enterprising approaches to their studies has helped to boost confidence and improved skills such as numeracy and decision-making. Support offered to schools that are performing less well and working with other highly successful schools has enhanced the professional development of staff and heightened their classroom effectiveness. A strong commitment to staff development has been a key component in ensuring that the school continues to improve at an impressive pace.

Strategy 3. Embedding the seven habits of highly effective teachers – and pupils

There are many other useful habits which, if encouraged and embedded, will certainly pay off in the long term in the classroom, whether or not Ofsted visits. Some of these are described below. They are useful for all teachers to develop in order to be the very best teachers they can be.

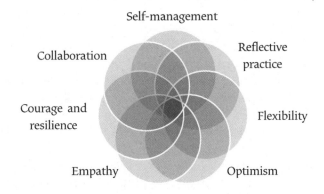

Many of the habits in this diagram overlap and interact with each other. They need to be developed in your teachers so they are constantly modelled for the pupils. This way, an emotionally intelligent ethos simply becomes 'the way we do things round here'.

Habit 1. Self-management

This includes all aspects of self-discipline for high levels of professional conduct. Punctuality is crucial, always arriving before the class (without coffee!). Punctuality with reports, replies and marking should also be a habit. Dressing appropriately will be even more important now that the head of Ofsted, Sir Michael Wilshaw, has mentioned that he expects it to be part of school policy. 'You look smart today Sir,' will be a most unwelcome compliment from friendly students!

Self-management needs to include managing the daily stresses and strains. Teaching is tough and demanding as well as rich and rewarding. Teachers need to grow a thick skin but still be sensitive and caring. Teachers need resilience so they can bounce back after being given a 'satisfactory' grading for a lesson they thought was 'good' or when a normally well-behaved class punishes a less inspiring moment with 'This is so boring' or 'I hate geography.' There is no teacher in the profession who hasn't had a tearful moment or woken up at 3 a.m. dreading Year 9 and considering imminent career change. A good self-manager accepts mistakes as learning experiences but works relentlessly to improve and impress both students and leaders.

Self-management also means:

■ Habitually checking for complacency whilst not beating yourself up when things don't go well each and every time

- Understanding about how the brain works so that when you panic or feel anxious, you realise this is normal and know that a trip to the gym or a long walk will make you feel better
- Taking care of your body and mind by eating healthy foods and reading books that challenge your thinking

Schools can promote self-management through its CPD programme, celebrations of individual achievements and a strict attendance, timekeeping and dress policy. Teachers are role models and professionals, so while there is room for individualism, school leaders will set the standards that reflect high aspirations. To me, respecting your role and your students means taking the time to look smart and show you care and, of course, this will be part of the picture an inspector paints of your school. Even more important though is the culture of mutual support, staffroom laughs and social events that promote a happy and hardworking community.

Habit 2. Reflective practice (metacognition)

Being a reflective practitioner is contagious. The habit of constantly reviewing how you can improve your teaching and the learning of your class means you will be flexible and responsive to children's needs. A trainer can easily spot a teaching staff that is habitually reflective. They are self-critical, curious, responsive and take away ideas to play with. They can stand back and analyse why they are responding in certain ways. They love to be challenged in their thinking and often relish the challenge of change. Reflective practitioners can reframe a situation and see it another way, and help students to do the same. For example, an inspection means having a chance to have our performance reflected back to us to show us how we are doing.

Getting your staff into the habit of reflection means helping them to accept that education will always be changing and that another initiative is another opportunity. Involving staff in the vision and distributing leadership to them all – even new teachers – will develop the habits of reflective practice.

Other important strategies that develop this habit include establishing learning groups or forums that focus on a school priority. Involve a mix of young, old, new, established, qualified and unqualified teachers in the groups. Give them a chance to lead training or run a student workshop to help establish and reward reflective practice. Run MBA courses and other teacher-led research, supported by and shared across the school. Mutual observation, coaching for all and students observing lessons also develop reflective practice.

Habit 3. Flexibility

Adapting to a changing world and ever-changing expectations is an essential habit for students and teachers. How can we help teachers to develop the habit of flexibility? A culture that values open-minded approaches to teaching and encourages risk-taking and creativity will facilitate flexible approaches to learning. Cross-curricular events, activity weeks, team teaching and a range of opportunities for staff to move outside their comfort zones will ensure they don't get too set in their ways and locked into their subject bunkers.

Flexibility is also developed through personal ownership of change, so coaching used at all levels as the culture for developing outstanding teaching and learning will ensure that teachers are constantly prodded to challenge themselves to find their own solutions.

Habit 4. Optimism

There is a four-letter word that is more important for learning than 'exam' and that is 'hope'. Teachers must believe their pupils can succeed in something. Children have to believe they can succeed in anything and be filled with hope and the expectation that they can make progress. A toddler wakes up every morning believing that he can and will learn new things. He will show a relentless optimism and determination to learn to walk, talk and find out about the world – until he is taught, or learns, to doubt himself and his abilities. Then everyone else starts constructing his learning.

Optimism about learning and having the potential to succeed are contagious. So are pessimism and negativity. There is plenty of research evidence to show that optimism can help us succeed (see Seligman 2011) and that creating a culture of optimism and hope in the classroom supports well-being. Some teachers believe that it is important to be 'realistic' rather than optimistic and that it's wrong to raise hopes that children can achieve more than we think they are capable of.

But do we know what they are capable of? How many children have achieved amazing things in their working lives even though they were a resounding 'failure' at school?

I once delivered an INSET at a school where everyone seemed to have a deeply held belief that any pupil can achieve an A – no matter how long it takes – if we find the right way to teach them. That school had the best value-added results in the country. Having the habit of optimism also helps develop the resilience essential for learning so that children can continually reframe failure as an opportunity to learn (for more on resilience see Habit 6).

Habit 5. Empathy

Empathy is part of our natural ability to really engage with other people's emotions and thereby understand their perspective on the world. Magnetic resonance imaging (MRI) scanning can now detect mirror neurons in our brains that light up when we respond to other people's emotions. This natural tendency to respond to others is the key to altruism and human benevolence. Most teachers go into the profession because they get a kick out of helping others succeed and find nothing more satisfying than having a challenging class and turning them on to learning.

There is another reason why empathy is a most important habit for exceptional teachers – empathetic people are very good at getting rapport. Rapport is that deep communication with a class or individual that elicits wonderful states of cooperation and motivation. It comes about through an ability to tune in to other people's interests. It's not just about what is said but *the way* it is said, so body language, intonation, register, eye contact and facial expression are all part of getting great rapport with a pupil or class. Knowing and understanding what they are interested in and being able to see the world from their viewpoint really helps to get great rapport with pupils – or any audience. Teachers who have high levels of empathy can get students on side and spread the culture of compassion that needs to underpin an 'outstanding' school community.

Habit 6. Courage and resilience

Being creative means breaking the rules – finding new solutions and pushing back the boundaries. This takes courage and confidence as it may go wrong – creativity is a risky business. We all have our comfort zones and these are part of our habitual behaviours, like sitting in the same seat in the staffroom, using the same coffee cup, teaching the same scheme of work and talking to the same colleagues. It feels good to be familiar and comfortable but exceptional teachers enjoy pushing themselves outside their comfort zones and helping students to do the same. You'll find out that we all learn best when we are a bit out of our depth and a bit scared. Being ambitious for your classes means having to try new ways of working, particularly for groups of children that don't learn easily.

Courage (along with optimism) helps you to be resilient. You need to be courageous to want to take advice and to seek out feedback from leaders, pupils, parents and colleagues about your performance. You then need the resilience to act on feedback – even when it isn't what you want to hear, bounce back and keep on trying to improve.

Habit 7. Collaboration

Human beings were born to collaborate and learn from each other. The very best teachers love to share ideas and resources and find a synergy in cross-fertilisation of ideas across departments and schools. Whether this is informal chat, a Twitter forum or attending conferences and subject workshops, being a good collaborator will enhance your teaching. If teachers can develop the habit of collaboration they will pick up the latest thinking, get involved in action research and ensure that students have transferable skills that make essential connections between subjects. Teachers who collaborate well will lead the general discourse around the school about the vision and values that make it outstanding.

Mentoring, buddying and/or coaching are essential to embed great learning across the school, so training staff about the importance of collaboration – rewarding and encouraging it – will make a big difference to the feel of school. Everything from staff karaoke or pantomimes to regular cross-curricular days and mixed staff INSET (from different subjects, phases, schools – mix as much as possible) encourage positive collaboration. We can never underestimate the influence of the 'movers and shakers' in the staff who are very good collaborators and who are always positive and optimistic. They influence the mood of the school. Effective collaborators are gold dust. They aren't always your heads of faculty but they are the staff members who organise the school social or quiz night and volunteer to lead twilight INSET when they have been on a course.

To foster better skills in collaboration, make coaching the core of your staff development programme. Learning coaching skills helps us learn to listen, develop empathy and experience the joy of helping someone else move forward and own their own changes. It is an opportunity too to use your more emotionally intelligent staff to gently coach others to move forward, improve their reflection and develop outstanding practice. For some previously successful teachers, set in didactic pedagogical ways, the move away from focusing on teaching to focusing on learning is a massive challenge to their self-esteem and their need to control the class. For an 'outstanding' judgement, lessons will have to demonstrate plenty of student-centred active learning. This means that coaching these highly intelligent, able teachers to transfer their talents to a facilitation model will be an essential transformation for many schools. The next chapter focuses on those 'outstanding' lessons.

Top tips

Here are some ideas from Wendy Briscoe, head teacher of Queen Victoria Primary School, a large primary school in Dudley.

- Spend time together with your staff wisely through giving them time to share good practice and generate good ideas. We regularly review our last Ofsted issues through staff producing a 'good tips sheet' at staff meetings. Teachers are also working on a framework and good advice for the top three strategies from the Sutton Trust's *Toolkit of Strategies to Improve Learning* (Higgins, Kokotsaki and Coe 2011) with the aim of feeding back to each other

- Give teachers opportunities to plan together. Planning, preparation and assessment time is given together as a year group every three weeks in our three form entry school

- Give the middle leaders time together to share the strengths and weaknesses in teaching and learning in their phases

- Engaging the skills and knowledge of the support staff about the children they work with is vital. We have research teams that include all the support staff to identify what the targeted group of children are finding difficult and then working on the issues and measuring the impact

- Involve your pupils in the 'coaching culture' as peer-assisted learning delivers many benefits for the tutor as well as the tutee. Also involve your pupils in a learning partnership with their teachers – let them 'lead their learning' through planning with the teacher for their learning experiences and encourage them to lead or deliver the lesson/parts of the lesson for their peers

- Make sure that teachers are given time to watch each other through a buddying system based on their strengths and development needs. Also let staff scrutinise each other's pupils' books

- Take your pupils and staff to other schools to observe teaching and learning

- Always allow your staff and pupils to take risks together and make learning exciting whatever they come up with! Let them make mistakes and learn from them. This builds confidence and motivation in the 'I can do' and breaks down the 'I can't do' culture

The habits of your pupils

The same seven habits of self-management, empathy, reflection, optimism, flexibility, courage/resilience and collaboration will help your pupils grow up to be as successful as they can be in our uncertain world. But how can we cultivate them in our students?

We all know that ultimately teaching is a game of bluff. If all the pupils decided to get up and walk out there is nothing we could do to stop them. They stay in our classrooms and at our schools by virtue of the tacit agreement that they want to be there. Let's not pretend it's just the law that keeps students coming to school. It is the fact that the critical mass of pupils (mostly) enjoys it because of the atmosphere that teachers create in every classroom, driven in turn by the leadership vision. The pupils have to be sold the vision too, so it has to relate to their lives and aspirations. An 'outstanding' school is one that feels like the students *want* to be there and are proud of their school. So their buy-in to the vision for the school is crucial.

Creating this positive culture comes from all teachers exemplifying and modelling the habits outlined above and helping the pupils 'catch' the same habits by making them believe in their own potential for successful learning. To support this culture, you need a mutually agreed, rigorous behaviour policy that is relentlessly consistent in its application by all staff – without any exceptions or deviations. Such policies, rigorously applied, create regular behaviours that become unconscious habits and expectations. Getting to lessons on time, with equipment, respecting each other and working hard are great habits that will be instilled by teachers with high expectations who know they have unconditional leadership back-up. It will also help to have an outstanding personal, social, health and economic (PSHE) education or learning to learn provision so that pupils can understand their brains, the nature of intelligence and (vitally) how to manage their thinking to keep mentally healthy and good at learning. 'Outstanding' schools have learners who have a language to discuss their learning and who do so – often.

This is the most reliable route to 'outstanding' behaviour. However, it is the minimum expectation in schools. Behaviour for learning goes beyond discipline and encompasses not only a behaviour policy that works but also children behaving in ways towards each other and the staff that really enhance their ability to learn. Working well independently and in groups, supporting each other's learning, asking good questions, taking the initiative more often and seeking feedback would characterise pupils with great learning behaviours. To achieve this it takes every adult in the school to reinforce the standards set and modelled by the leadership team – even on wet, windy days at the end of term.

Don't underestimate the vital importance of 'tutor time' and PSHE education. School leaders are aware that the secondary class tutor or primary class teacher can have a huge impact on a pupil's progress and attitude. The strong relationship, constant encouragement, informal feedback and rapport that is formed with a class can be the key to success for the vulnerable pupil who has a difficult home background. Ensuring that staff are trained to be as good as they can be at giving this personal support and enhancing this with a powerful PSHE programme delivered with enthusiasm is the mark of an 'outstanding' school. Assemblies and cross-curricular activities are the ideal vehicle to embed the values and vision of the school. An inspector will soak up all these aspects of your hidden curriculum and expect to see its impact on the students around the school. Bear in mind that if your inspection is finely balanced, SMSC (spiritual, moral, social and cultural) development will be a deciding factor.

> An important aspect of the overall effectiveness of judgement is a consideration of how well the school contributes to the promotion of the pupils' spiritual, moral, social and cultural development.
>
> Ofsted, *Subsidiary Guidance Supporting the Inspection of Maintained Schools and Academies* (2012): 23

Strategy 4. Getting middle leaders to buy in

The hardest job in the school is faculty or department leader, particularly in the core subjects. They take the flak from above and below. But they are the torchbearers of your school vision and will drive the embedding of the values and strategies agreed at leadership level – or not. The middle leaders lead the teams that deliver in the classroom. Their skills as leaders and practitioners will determine the performance of each department and thereby the performance of the school.

Leaders are judged by the performance of those they are responsible for but many middle leaders don't really realise this or accept that accountability. Have you ever heard a head of department say '*My* results were OK, though ...' when challenged on underperformance in their department?

In contrast, outstanding middle leaders really understand accountability and make it their mission in life to build their subject performance and know exactly the strengths and weaknesses of their team. They have a regular rigorous programme of observation and work scrutiny but also can give expert support as coaches and mentors, which can empower individual teachers with confidence and resilience. Performance management is a high priority in the 2012 inspection schedule and outstanding middle leaders play a lead role in making it effective in their departments. This includes deciding to recommend capability procedures when necessary. They know their own subject data inside out and can give a regular update of progress at any time during the year. They know the school priorities and the underperforming groups so they can address these in their schemes and plans. They can analyse exam results and talk about the individual performance of teachers or of pupils on certain questions in an exam.

Under the new inspection framework, middle leaders may well find themselves being more actively engaged during an inspection through possible joint lesson observation. Middle leadership is also judged through meetings with them, seeing department self-evaluation documents and discussion with the SLT on the roles of middle leaders. Their evaluations of middle leaders' input can make an important contribution to the overall judgements inspectors reach, particularly on leadership. So the middle leaders have never been so important – not just for the inspection, but because good middle leaders will facilitate sustainable school improvement, embed best practice and help ensure better outcomes for all children in the school.

Essential features of successful long-term middle leadership include:

- Leadership training for all those in leadership roles, especially those who have just been appointed. This should include: creating your vision, managing data to close the achievement gap, coaching skills, managing your team, performance management, lesson observation, emotional intelligence and outstanding learning

- Every middle leader to produce their own concise departmental self-evaluation form after results publication and present a summary to the SLT and governors. This should include analysis of performance in terms of individual groups, teachers, exam papers, coursework options and an action plan to address current needs

- Every middle leader to observe lessons in their own and other subjects, alongside a member of the SLT, as training for any inspection and to broaden their understanding of learning and progress

- Every middle leader to scrutinise books in their department and report on progress over time each term

- Middle leaders to rotate on annual secondment to the SLT so that they can see the way school priorities are discussed

- Middle leaders to visit other schools, including cross-phase options, as part of their performance management and to report on the learning seen to take forward with their teams. This will ensure that they stay alert to developments outside their own school setting

- Set up a middle leadership group with specific responsibilities for planning INSET to help them deliver the training needs for their teams

---

[Inspectors should have] a clear focus on the quality of middle leaders in a school.

Ofsted, *Subsidiary Guidance Supporting the Inspection of Maintained Schools and Academies* (2012): 13

Strategy 5. Ensuring effective performance management and continuous professional development

At every school there is a range of experience and effectiveness amongst teachers. The school's strategy for continuous improvement has to involve both performance management

(PM) and continuing professional development (CPD) to meet the expressed needs of all teachers and deliver 'good' or 'outstanding' teaching. PM and CPD should also be focused on developing the habits of highly effective teachers described above.

To make sure that the SLT and middle leaders can effectively measure the impact of training and consistently judge the standard of teaching, they will need to be trained in lesson observation. They will also need instruction in coaching staff for improvement. In addition, schools will need to train up their senior and middle leaders to observe alongside inspectors, so that they can provide a check and balance to judgements. This is particularly important where inspectors are not subject specialists. Your staff need to be able to argue cogently about judgements made based on evidence seen in the lessons. So be aware that inspectors will be:

> observing some lessons jointly with senior staff before discussing them also with the teacher who has been observed [and] discussing teaching and learning with staff.
>
> Ofsted, *Evaluation Schedule for the Inspection of Maintained Schools and Academies* (2012): 12

PM that is flexible and revisited frequently is a driving force for school improvement.

Teachers regularly need to ask students about their own teaching and its effectiveness and feed this into their own PM. This can be done through questionnaires or by the head of department meeting pupils. The results should be discussed at meetings with the department head in an open and honest way.

As the figure above suggests, studying the PM of staff should give clear insights into the real school priorities for training and staff development. It should be fed into the school self-evaluation form and used to help drive the school priorities forward. Too often though, PM is a paper exercise that has little impact on school improvement and CPD is unfocused. Set up a spreadsheet of all the observations completed over the year, all RAG rated (Red for unsatisfactory, Amber for borderline and Green for good/outstanding) to show who has needed extra support and coaching and for what. This is evidence that you have an excellent tracking system for assessing teacher performance. Put it alongside your performance management information that shows training needs and what action is taken when teachers need to improve.

Ensure that your PM and CPD deliver a measurable impact on outcomes and link very clearly to the school development plan. Also, keep evidence of just what justification you have for teachers moving up the pay scale, as monitoring this aspect of PM is on the horizon.

Strategy 6. Engaging with the whole school community

The 2012 evaluation schedule stresses that inspectors will triangulate their judgements using other sources such as discussions with pupils and taking account of parents' or carers' views. The latter is made possible through the online questionnaire Parent View. This also signposts parents on how to make a complaint or raise further issues. So – be proactive! Set up your own forum in advance so that you really know what is being said out there and can deal with it. It is a crucial part of your school self-evaluation. (See Kayembe 2008 for suggestions.)

Engagement with parents and carers is a key issue for any school and we should try to find new and effective ways to involve the most reluctant. Parenting workshops can be a successful way to develop engagement for all age groups and could give you a pool of parents to choose from to meet a future inspection team. Whatever you do, create an evidence trail to show how you have dealt with any concerns – very useful to show to inspectors!

In their evaluation of quality of teaching, inspectors will be:

> discussing pupils' work with them and their experience of teaching and learning over longer periods
>
> [and] taking account of the views of pupils, parents and carers, and staff.
>
> Ofsted, *Evaluation Schedule for the Inspection of Maintained Schools and Academies* (2012): 12

Case study: Developing a culture and ethos for 'outstanding'

At the core of all our work is relationships, relationships, relationships.

John Wells, head teacher, Clevedon School

Clevedon School is a large secondary in Bristol with an average intake of students who need to have higher aspirations. The school has travelled the rocky road from a 'notice to improve' in 2004, to 'satisfactory' in 2009, to 'outstanding' in its 2011 Ofsted inspection. When you walk around the school there is a tangible air of excitement and absolute pride in what they have become and in where it could go from here.

The head teacher, John Wells, wrote the Ofsted report he wanted to see six months before the last inspection in the form of headline comments that linked every aspect to the criteria for 'outstanding'. This 'report' was presented to staff with the comment: 'Can we jump from satisfactory to outstanding?' He had planted the seed that this might be possible. He wanted to develop strength and depth in teaching and learning. To aid this, all lesson observations monitored by senior staff are interactive learning experiences where teachers are encouraged to discuss how they are targeting vulnerable students during the lesson. The observer feeds back what he or she can see happening in the lesson and coaches for the little adjustments that will help with the progress for all students. The SLT has developed a dynamic and innovative CSPD (continuous self-professional development) programme which is highly responsive to staff action research.

The head teacher set up Vision Groups after the 'satisfactory' grade in 2009 to help staff drive forward the priorities of the school. The staff working groups have been highly effective in driving forward strategies based on school needs, for example tutoring, personal, learning and thinking skills (PLTS), outstanding learning and gender issues. The Vision Groups have been given the space, time and resources to drill down into problems, come up with solutions and then to lead training sessions to address needs. The Vision Groups involve volunteers from across the school drawn from both teaching and non-teaching staff. The next stage is to involve students.

A wide range of innovations have developed from this very inclusive approach to school development such as:

- Vertical tutor groups that create a real sense of a caring community
- House systems that drive this pastoral system and lead to many cross-curricular activities and challenges

- Amazing assemblies produced by children and a constant stream of cross-phase community projects owned and delivered by students

Now they are developing 'home learning' through planners that are soon to be replaced by iPads for every student. It is hoped this will further engage parents through the learning platform and interactive homework.

The assistant head in charge of teaching and learning spent the morning of the Ofsted inspection cycling the Downs at 3 a.m. because he felt *so* excited about the SLT being able to show off what the school staff had achieved. This spirit is contagious at Clevedon School because everyone wants to be observed! There is a confidence amongst staff to take risks and try out exciting active learning pedagogy. This has been the fruit of a distributed leadership of training and an innovative approach to observation which nurtures self-awareness through constant filming of student responses. The films are later used in feedback sessions to show teachers what learning is or is not taking place. Teachers were banging on the door to get observed during my visit – a major transformation from the closed-door policy of a decade before.

On the first day of the inspection in October 2011, the head teacher proudly told his story of the school's development. He knew his data inside out and back to front, so he made it easy for the Ofsted team to get answers on how he was (and is) closing any perceived gaps. But he also conveyed at every opportunity what Clevedon is about. He made sure that the inspectors knew about the students and the staff having a 'passion to improve' and, most importantly, their genuine belief that they can and will make a huge difference in every classroom across the school.

John is a powerful, persuasive man with a gentle charisma and over the next few days, as he unveiled the very best of Clevedon for them to observe, the inspection team said: 'We have never seen a school like this before.' They had seen something 'outstanding' – not just the data, not just the teaching and learning, but the whole culture and ethos of collaborative improvement which means that Clevedon will continue onward and upward.

What do the students think? I asked a Year 8 girl on the reception desk what she liked most about Clevedon. Without hesitation she said: 'They are preparing us for our future.'

Strategy 7. Rigorous self-evaluation – know thyself!

The self-evaluation form (SEF) is dead. Long live the SEF!

One of the very best things seen in many 'outstanding' schools in the last five years has been the process of rigorous self-evaluation at all levels within the school organisation. Although it is no longer compulsory to file a SEF online, inspectors will expect to see a (concise) summary of it (Ofsted 2012a: 18). Your SEF is still your most important tool for improvement. Now we can tailor this process to suit ourselves. This section makes some suggestions drawn from schools with the very best practice. An example of self evaluation practice from Eliot Primary School in London can be found on the Ofsted good practice website (www. goodpractice.ofsted.gov.uk/downloads/documents/Eliot_ Bank_Good_Practice_Example.pdf).

The principle purpose of self-evaluation is that you know your school well enough to be able to write your own school inspection report. Your challenge is to write your own Ofsted report six months before they come, so that when they arrive they don't have to change a word!

John Wells from Clevedon School wrote the report he wanted six months before Ofsted arrived. Having had a surprise 'satisfactory' report twelve months previously he wanted staff to be absolutely clear what he expected. But first he had to know exactly the strengths and weaknesses of his school – and what was everyone doing to address them – and make any crucial changes.

360 degree self-awareness

This means being willing to expose yourself and your school to compliments or criticism from every angle. For many years Ofsted have been triangulating the judgements schools make about themselves with what students say in meetings, what the middle leaders say about school priorities and what parents say about how they feel the school deals with issues raised. This is being taken to a new level with the Parent View website (www.parentview.ofsted.gov.uk/) which allows parents to communicate online about their child's school.

[Parent View is] a new online questionnaire that will allow parents and carers to give their views on their child's school at any time of the year. Covering over 22,000 schools across England, the 12-question survey will help other parents as they make important choices about their child's education and provide Ofsted with information about schools that will help inform priorities for inspection.

Parent View has been produced with the assistance of a panel of parents who contributed to shaping the questions and the way the site functions. The questionnaire covers a range of topics, including quality of teaching, bullying, behaviour and levels of homework, allowing parents to give a view about their child's school on each issue, with a final question as to whether or not they would recommend the school to other parents. The questionnaire does not allow free text comments but invites responses to a series of closed questions.

The questions were carefully chosen to cover those issues that parents told Ofsted are the most important to them. They are also designed to provide Ofsted with the information to support decisions about inspection and will give headteachers a direct route into gathering the views of their parent group.

Ofsted, 'A New Voice for Parents' (2011)

Submissions to Parent View will form part of the risk assessment process Ofsted use to decide if your school should be inspected sooner rather than later, so it is high stakes for many of us. This means that you need to set up your own school forum for parents – so that you can see what the issues or concerns are and address them before they come up on the public forum.

The aim of 360 degree self-awareness is an intention to really listen to *all* stakeholders. So you also need a student forum which meets regularly with the head or SLT to express their views or concerns. This allows you to show that you listen and demonstrate what is being done to address the concerns. It doesn't necessarily mean agreeing to requests for less homework but it can generate a record of issues that show a trail of actions and outcomes. This is very helpful if parents suggest you don't listen or respond – you can show that, actually, you do.

Staff also need opportunities to feed back to the head and SLT about how well they are led and managed. This can be built into the performance management process described in Strategy 5.

Too often, leaders in a school don't always know the school's real needs because their processes for self-evaluation are not driven by a determination to get feedback on everything. Frequently there is an inability to take constructive criticism without taking offence. The principle of 'There is no such thing as failure – only feedback' should drive PM and 360 degree self-awareness.

The table on pages 46–47 (based on the Johari window) helps us understand why a school needs to be relentlessly diligent in seeking out feedback from all. The Open window is the one open to the outside world and is the one we are judged on. But it is the job of an Ofsted inspection team to pry into the Blind and Hidden quadrants to see if we know about them and, if so, what we are doing about the issues in them. The Unknown quadrant contains things that may happen that we just don't know about yet. However, if we have staff keeping abreast of the latest news from the

Department for Education and who are engaged in activities such as writing learning research projects as part of our CPD, then we have a good chance of being ahead of the game. The idea of this model is that you should try to expand the Open/ Public quadrant to take in as much of the Blind and Hidden quadrants as possible by having systems that feed back to you exactly what people think.

For example, your school reception desk is the first contact a visitor has with your school. Do you know how it affects visitors? As a frequent visitor to schools I can tell so much about the quality of the school from that first impression. How quickly are you attended to? How pleasant is the recep- tionist? How positive and child-centred is the waiting area? In short, how well does the area reflect the school's vision and culture? For Ofsted inspectors this is also their first con- tact with the school. They will be thinking immediately: 'Does this feel outstanding?'

Open/Public

- School office reception
- Other public areas of the school
- School website
- Parent View
- Published exam results
- Actions and appearance of students (and staff) on the way to school and outside
- School inspection report
- Vision and mission statements
- Policies

(Can be) Hidden

- Performance details of certain subjects or teachers
- Financial risks
- Unmanageable students
- Less capable teachers or ineffective leaders
- Incompetent governors
- Missing or ineffective policies
- Lack of challenge or support from governors
- Stroppy parents
- Underperforming vulnerable groups (especially if very small in number)

Blind

- School gate rumour
- Community perception
- Other schools' opinions
- Staffroom 'jungle telegraph'
- Unseen/unreported bullying
- Poor practice behind closed classroom doors

Unknown

- Next inspection report
- Hidden potential of staff and students
- Future demographic changes
- Possible government diktats and policies
- Future developments in neuroscience that influence learning

Strategy 8. Using the self-evaluation form to produce a live school development plan

The results of the self-evaluation will form the basis of your development plan. Both documents should be regularly updated, fed by all departments and leaders throughout the school and be responsive to any new data. A good school development plan (SDP) will show that your school listens to its staff, students and parents, knows its priorities and can demonstrate that you have the paper trail to show what you are doing about it.

Many schools find from their SEF that they need to include the following in their SDPs and then make them happen:

- Ensure that performance management is an effective part of the self-evaluation process
- Ensure that governors are encouraged to use the SEF to challenge and support the school
- Ensure that the chair writes a brief SEF on the work of the governors
- Include an immediate evaluation of the quality of literacy and numeracy delivery across the school with a programme for improvement
- Arrange training for teaching assistants (TAs) in literacy, Assessment for Learning and metacognitive strategies to overcome barriers to learning

- Be prepared to review staffing if any TAs are not able to deliver top quality support
- Create a forum for parents and students to give their opinions and to respond to their concerns

A good SEF often reveals issues about whether your tracking data is accurate and is effectively used to measure progress. It is not just a paper exercise. Clearer focus is often needed on the progress of vulnerable or underachieving groups of students. Many schools put a member of the SLT in charge of personally tracking these groups. They also ensure that all middle leaders are tracking progress in every class and that all assessment data is moderated across other schools.

Governors have an even more important role now that schools have freedom from local authority stewardship. They need accurate information about the strengths and weaknesses of the school through the SEF. They also need to produce their own SEF, which demonstrates what their strengths and weaknesses are and how they are addressing them. This is discussed and minuted in meetings and will skill them up to have the conversations they will need to have with future inspection teams.

If you have a live SDP, based on a reliable SEF, you could write your own Ofsted report today and then put plans in place to make your school outstanding tomorrow.

Chapter 2
Learning in lessons

[T]eachers, schools, and systems need to be consistently aware and have dependable evidence of the effects they are having on their students and from this evidence make the decisions about how they teach and what they teach. The message is that the evidence is about student learning – particularly progress – provided that the learning intentions and success criteria are worthwhile, challenging, and become meaningful to and understood by the students.

John Hattie, *Visible Learning for Teachers* (2012)

The quality of a school is largely reflected in the quality of its teaching. When judging teaching, we shall revise the criteria for judging the effectiveness of teaching and concentrate more on direct observation of teaching and learning. This will help inspectors to judge even more perceptively the quality of teaching in the school and its impact on pupils' learning and progress.

Ofsted, *Inspection 2012: Proposals for Inspection Arrangements for Maintained Schools and Academies* (2011): 11

Every teacher is likely to be observed at least once. This should be taken as an opportunity to show off the work of the school and defy the number-crunchers by demonstrating the high quality of teaching and learning that exists throughout the school. Performance data may give a quantitative account of outcomes but the observation of teaching will truly tell the story of your school. Making observations a success story is the result of good leadership of the pedagogy, training, behaviour management and environment in your school. Together these build a consistent culture of determination amongst staff to grow great learners and amongst pupils to become great learners. This chapter outlines some practical advice about how to deliver tremendous lessons that help pupils make good progress every day.

A close look at the 2012 guidance can help you plan strategies that will ensure that high expectations and great learning are embedded and become 'the way we always do things round here' – not just for inspection day. This will become obvious to inspectors and ensure the right boxes are ticked on the judgement sheets.

There will be a closer, focused scrutiny of the way the school meets the individual needs of students such as those with disabilities, special educational needs, English as an additional language (EAL), young carers and those from low incomes. They will look for any potential underachievement amongst these groups and amongst others such as boys, girls, ethnic minorities or the academically able.

Any gaps between the school outcomes and national average outcomes for pupils, especially vulnerable pupils, must be seen to be narrowing rapidly. This means that leaders and teachers must have accurate information about the progress of all of these students, and in the classroom these students need to be seen to be making the most progress. We must show we know the needs within each class (not just as a list) and have long-term plans to monitor and meet their changing needs. This will involve the use of additional resources, planned involvement of TAs and quality oral and written feedback to students (and their parents).

The ingredients of your 'outstanding' lesson should include the following ten attributes:

1. Engagement

The 'primacy effect' suggests that first impressions are so powerful that they can override objective judgements. The primacy effect for your students occurs in the first six seconds of your lesson. In an observation the first six seconds of an inspector's visit to your classroom will be influential. Getting brains engaged immediately pays massive dividends. A class enthusiastically involved in learning is incredibly impressive, so engagement from the very start of the lesson is vital.

To achieve this you must engage the pupils' emotional brains through novelty, humour, mystery, variety, intrigue, challenge, puzzle, enthusiasm or music. Ensure students engage immediately with lesson objectives by asking questions like: 'What will change if we meet this objective?', 'What questions do you want to ask about this objective?', 'How will we really know we have met it?', 'Can you find ten crazy ways to show me you have succeeded in this objective?' and 'What is the first thing I need to do this lesson?'

You could simply start the lesson and then get them to guess the objective or break out of your usual routine of PowerPoint, lesson objective, activate, demonstrate, plenary. Change can also be effective for engagement.

Remember, when an observer talks to students later in the lesson about what they are doing, the conversation will seek to find out just how far they have engaged with and understood your lesson objectives.

2. Challenge and feedback

It isn't enough to say your expectations are high – you have to encourage a culture within your classroom that says, 'In here we all support each other to work beyond our comfort zone.' Do your students know what their 'comfort' and 'challenge' zones are and that they should be working in the latter? Have they got a habit of pushing themselves when work gets hard or dull? Do they understand that some learning needs lots of repetition to get it right? Having high expectations of individuals with various needs requires accurate assessment of potential barriers to learning, then having challenging targets that make the child aim higher.

A sense of challenge should be clear in your feedback also. Research has found effective feedback to be one of the most profound and powerful ways to close the gap for under-achievers (see Higgins, Kokotsaki and Coe 2011). Are you good at giving effective feedback? (If you aren't sure ask your students!)

Remember, inspectors will be evaluating:

> how well pupils understand how to improve their learning as a result of frequent, detailed and accurate feedback from teachers following assessment of their learning.
>
> Ofsted, *Evaluation Schedule for the Inspection of Maintained Schools and Academies* (2012): 11

Oral or written feedback that is specific and positive and that guides students to make progress in their learning journey is both developmental and motivational.

Specific and positive feedback needs to be present in students' books and in the classroom dialogue, otherwise students can become demotivated, confused or misled.

Feedback can also include peer-assessment, but make sure that your students are trained to make it positive and specific. To ensure that the students read it, all written feedback should include MRI (My Response Is.) This means that the student has to read what you have written before writing their response and commitment to follow the advice. (Thanks to the teacher I recently trained who gave me this one!)

Inspectors will evaluate:

> the extent to which the pace and depth of learning are maximised as a result of teachers' monitoring of learning during lessons and any consequent actions in response to pupils' feedback.
>
> Ofsted, *Evaluation Schedule for the Inspection of Maintained Schools and Academies* (2012): 11

3. Questioning

Asking questions is the bread and butter of teaching. Using questions to develop learning and help students make progress in their thinking is a subject in itself. Good, open, engaging questions promote thinking at the highest hierarchical levels in Bloom's Taxonomy (creativity and evaluation). Questions like 'why', 'how' and 'what if' are the basic tools of teaching. But we should also make students formulate more of their own questions more often, encourage thinking time for questions and use methods such as Philosophy for Children's Community of Enquiry (see www.sapere.org.uk). These raise the amount of student dialogue in a lesson and, as the average verbal expression for a student in a secondary classroom is only five words, this has to be a priority.

Questions that students ask can also act as a form of plenary to measure learning.

The beauty of students constructing questions instead of lots of answers is that questions, unlike answers, can't be easily defined as right or wrong, giving a freedom to explore and deepen learning. For example, you could say: 'Think of three questions this article raises' or 'Tell me three things you have learnt from this article.' Both measure your progress but feel very different. This technique could help address both of the following evaluations:

- the extent to which teachers' questioning and use of discussion promotes learning
- the extent to which teachers enthuse, engage and motivate pupils to learn and foster their curiosity and enthusiasm for learning.

Ofsted, *Evaluation Schedule for the Inspection of Maintained Schools and Academies* (2012): 11

---

4. Independent learning

This is still a focus for inspection teams. Spoonfed students who have not developed research or thinking skills and who have been scaffolded through the tests are notorious at all levels. Doing it for them is so much easier than teaching them to do it for themselves. But this type of 'learning' is shallow and short lived. Deeper learning needs the purpose of the learning to be explained and active engagement and involvement with the material to make proper progress.

Building up good collaborative learning practice and rewarding individual initiative has to be part of school policy and now it must be embedded in lessons to be able to demonstrate it on inspection day. We also need to encourage the transfer of skills and linking of knowledge across subjects and across home/school/work boundaries.

5. Embed the teaching of core skills – especially literacy – in all lessons

Knowing your subject and how to help pupils make lasting progress in subject-related skills is the mark of an expert teacher. Delivering this progress, and enhancing the core skills of literacy, oracy, ICT and numeracy, are now also essential. This means taking every opportunity to connect classroom learning to the real world, modelling expert core skills and correcting mistakes relentlessly.

A focus on core skills is particularly prominent in the new evaluation schedule. If your school's literacy outcomes are less than expected, expect an even sharper focus. Inspectors will evaluate:

how well teaching enables pupils to develop skills in reading, writing, communication and mathematics.

Ofsted, *Evaluation Schedule for the Inspection of Maintained Schools and Academies* (2012): 11

It is entirely appropriate that there is an emphasis on literacy and numeracy. We know that without these skills, access to the rest of the curriculum and prospects in the world of work are limited. The concern about the lack of numeracy and literacy skills in young people (even those who get GCSE English at C grade) has been well rehearsed recently. For years we have been trying to give our students the skills to function well as employees and citizens, but all the statistics show we have actually failed miserably. Too many leave school lacking essential skills.

A single literacy or numeracy coordinator in schools putting up subject 'key words' in every classroom will no longer suffice. Teaching core skills is not a job only for the English or maths departments either. Every teacher in every lesson must make a contribution to improving them. The core skills must be taught and *modelled* right across the curriculum. We need to be more creative and ambitious in creating strategies that improve these skills in new and exciting ways, in every classroom, from Reception to Year 13.

An exciting, ongoing, rigorous literacy and numeracy drive (starting with the teachers) encompassing every aspect of school life must aim for better outcomes. This means building a more 'hearts and minds' determination by students and teachers to first value and then develop core skills in a less prescriptive way than the Literacy Strategy. Many schools have done it – even those with large EAL and special needs intakes. These schools are places where there are effective programmes for meeting additional needs and where core skills happen in every classroom. They value and reward high quality 'writing to inform or persuade' in every subject and have teachers who themselves have high level core skills and who model them consistently – no excuses. Students also have their own core skills leadership teams and champion communication skills because they know that they matter.

The grade descriptor for 'inadequate' teaching (in part) says:

> Pupils cannot communicate, read, write or use mathematics as well as they should.
>
> Ofsted, *Evaluation Schedule for the Inspection of Maintained Schools and Academies* (2012): 14

Where appropriate in lessons, try to refer to other core skills but remember that literacy is *the* core skill that can and must be taught and modelled in every lesson. In secondary schools, the development of literacy will be expected in every subject. In primary, literacy will be a focus in all subjects but with the additional focus on phonics, reading, writing and oracy, especially between the ages of 4 to 7. In addition, numeracy is a key focus for primary schools across the curriculum (see Ofsted 2012c: 13–14). Delivering progress in literacy in your lesson will be expected if you are to be rated 'outstanding'. So where do we start?

First, ensure that *your* literacy skills are perfect. Check your spelling and grammar in every PowerPoint or written word you place on the board or wall. Get into the habit of getting it right – every time. (As a frequent lesson observer, I find at least 50% of teachers make literacy errors.) We can't be 'perfect' all the time but we must try to be. There are no excuses – you *must* model excellence. If you aren't confident, insist your school runs a course for teachers who need help.

To have a 'literate' lesson, make sure that you:

- Build literacy into your lesson plan
- Introduce new vocabulary (not just subject-related words)
- Value reading and encourage paired, private and reading aloud in class
- Give wider subject reading suggestions, including relevant magazines
- Give tips on paragraphing, spelling, punctuation and grammar

- Reward literacy skills used in your lessons

- Encourage the use of Standard English rigorously, both spoken and written. When it is appropriate not to use it say why (e.g. in role play)

- Reinforce grammatical accuracy in spoken language (e.g. correcting 'We was ...')

- Use texting, Twitter, email and so on to emphasise a variety of formats and their strengths and weaknesses as good communication skills in your subject

- Care about literacy skills in your lesson – offer prizes for students who catch you out making a mistake and model mistakes as learning experiences

- Remind students about writing in good clear sentences and paragraphs – if you show you value this, they will value it too

- Look out for students who are not reading very much because others in the group are doing it for them

- Mark spellings and give spelling tests for subject-related words

- Give students an opportunity to assess their writing skills using a simple grid whenever they do any written work

- Ensure key terms and vocabulary are clearly explained – and related to similar words or their root

- Give regular advice on spelling and punctuation strategies

- Enhance skills in skimming and scanning text for information

■ Explain writing conventions as part of your delivery (e.g. writing to inform or persuade)

Finally, have you ever noticed that some students don't like to read and write? They are the very students who need to read and write more often in your lesson. More reading and more writing is crucial for improvement in literacy.

Top tips

Here are some suggestions from Rupert Prutton, assistant head teacher at Fulston Manor in Kent.

■ Ensure the students are active learners, not passive – keep them busy

■ Scaffold the tasks and instructions so every student knows the required information – task *and* theory – so everything is very clear

■ Build a consistently positive working environment – quality Assessment for Learning will help do this

■ Have confidence to be creative in the approaches you take to student-led tasks – try out new ideas

■ Be reflective and gather as much feedback as possible on lessons – always be open to remodelling your teaching

■ Ensure that literacy doesn't become a barrier to learning by being aware of student needs – how do you communicate with students and how do they communicate with each other?

- Use pace and effective classroom management to support the students' learning - keep the students focused on the learning
- Build confidence in all students through the use of skills and praise - ensure aspiration in students is very strong
- Be aware of students' needs and capabilities in order to make learning accessible to all
- Have fun learning with the students - otherwise you will all get bored!

6. Mind the gap! Progress for all – and especially those who need it most

Seeing engaged, resilient, ambitious learners working independently in the classroom on challenging activities and making *good* or *outstanding progress* will still be the mark of an 'outstanding' lesson. But there are aspects of judgements in the 2012 evaluation schedule that will be useful to build into your lessons.

Make sure you know where the attainment gaps in your classes are and that you plan *every* lesson to help those pupils make *extra* progress. It is likely inspectors may track such students to see how their needs are being addressed. While on site inspectors will also evaluate:

the extent to which the education provided meets the needs of the range of pupils at the school, and in particular, the needs of disabled pupils and those who have special educational needs.

Ofsted, *The Framework for School Inspection* (2012): 14

[Inspectors will also consider]

how well disabled pupils and those who have special educational needs have achieved since joining the school

how well gaps are narrowing between the performance of different groups of pupils in the school and compared to all pupils nationally

how well pupils make progress relative to their starting points.

Ofsted, *The Framework for School Inspection* (2012): 14

Part of closing achievement gaps is to use teaching assistants (the most expensive resource in the classroom after the teacher) effectively to help all pupils progress and close the gap in attainment. Research has shown that TAs don't always increase the progress of students they work with, so expect a focus on this aspect of your lesson.

Your special educational needs coordinator should provide clear guidance about the starting points of all the children with special needs/statements, so it is clear what progress they have made at the school.

Top tips for improving your use of TAs include ensuring that:

- They know and understand the objectives of the lesson – and how they relate to the students they are working with
- You have planned for their input and made a note of this in your plan
- They understand progression in your subject and how to scaffold it
- They have a way to feed back to you the successes and failures of the learning – linked to the objectives of that lesson
- They can mark and set targets linked to progression and objectives for their students
- They help students to set success criteria and understand exactly what they need to do
- They can assess and observe – giving the one-to-one feedback that really works
- They believe they can make a difference to progress
- They are your eyes and ears in terms of identifying progress problems and what *you* need to do next
- You keep a record of the way they are contributing to learning over time

Case study

Head teacher Julie Summerfield, of Horndean Technology College in Hampshire, shares an extract from her strategic plan for improving teaching and learning at her school.

Strategic whole college leadership

▪ **Increase in observation and observation types:**
There has been a clear directive that subject leaders (or their delegate) *must* formally observe each member of their department at least once per term. Additionally, subject leaders, year leaders, advanced skills teachers (ASTs)/advanced teachers (ATs) and senior leaders are carrying out learning walks and 'drop-in' observations on a regular basis. This means we have a large database of evidence regarding the quality of teaching.

▪ **Comprehensive tracking of the quality of teaching and learning and the 'Dashboard':** All lesson observations, whether formal or informal, are tracked on a comprehensive spreadsheet. This means we can gauge the overall quality of teaching very easily and interrogate the data to look at subjects or individuals. The data can also be used to compare gradings given by staff in different roles to see if there is any bias. This information is summarised in graphical and tabular form using the Teaching and

Learning Dashboard, a document that is updated from live data every time it is opened.

■ **Deputy head teacher and assistant head teacher (AHT) review every observation and identify areas to improve:** The director of teaching and head teacher review all lesson observation feedback forms to identify, discuss and formulate actions to address any common areas that need to be developed.

■ **AST/AHT work with a consultant to develop the use of learning objectives and ways to demonstrate progress:** The director of teaching and a head teacher consultant AST have worked for a day with a strategy consultant to begin to unpick how to develop and address some of the development areas identified through observation.

Strategic whole college leadership/leadership of subject leaders

■ **Teaching and learning self-evaluation against criteria for Ofsted outstanding lessons:** The director of teaching led the team of ASTs and ATs in the research and production of a self-evaluation document that would allow teachers to evaluate their own practice, scoring themselves against the criteria for an outstanding lesson. This information has then been collated into a single spreadsheet so staff training needs can be easily identified.

■ **Teaching and learning self-evaluation used to direct a peer observation programme which is focused and linked to performance management:** The evaluation document allowed staff to reflect on their practice and identify a suitable focus for observations of their peers. Each member of staff will observe three other members of staff, at least one of which has been selected for having strength in the area of focus of the observing teacher.

■ **Scheme of work monitoring:** Monitoring of long-term planning and modelling the format of long-term plans will drive up standards and model good lesson structure and content.

■ **Line management focus on student progress and quality of teaching and learning:** Line management meetings have an agenda set by the director of teaching. These have a focus on progress, teaching and learning and include a half-termly learning walk so that the line manager and subject leader can review the quality of teaching together and compare and calibrate judgements.

■ **Judgements and evidence of quality of teaching and learning linked to the monitoring calendar:** The monitoring calendar has more emphasis on the quality of teaching and learning. This is also reflected in the new monitoring calendars for ATs and ASTs.

7. Use assessment to support effective learning

Ensuring that teachers accurately assess and effectively plan the next steps for individual students will still be monitored in the 2012 evaluation schedule. But effective feedback that supports continuing progress, based on accurate assessment, is a crucial aspect of outstanding teaching (see Higgins, Kokotsaki and Coe 2011). Feedback must be focused exactly on what the student has to do to make progress. Clear, focused advice about how to progress must be evident in scrutinised books and oral feedback.

Teachers must ask questions in the classroom that help students find new strategies when they get stuck and help them relish the challenge of learning from mistakes. Exceptional teaching will also involve training your students to give and take constructive criticism from their peers to support each other's progress. Do some of this peer teaching and learning every lesson – with or without an observer.

Active learning and group work are 80% of a 'perfect' lesson, so use this time with individual pupils to systematically and effectively check understanding. Make sure your interventions and those of any other adult have a real impact on quality of learning and progress.

Part of the grade descriptor for 'outstanding' teaching says:

Marking and constructive feedback from both teacher and pupils are frequent and of a consistently high quality, which enables pupils to understand how to improve their work, encouraging high levels of interest and engagement.

Ofsted, *Evaluation Schedule for the Inspection of Maintained Schools and Academies* (2012): 13

8. Subject expertise and progress in the subject

Good and outstanding teaching combines strong subject knowledge with effective teaching of the skills needed and a thorough understanding of what pupils already know:

Drawing on excellent subject knowledge, teachers plan astutely and set challenging tasks based on systematic, accurate assessment of pupils' prior skills, knowledge and understanding.

Ofsted, *Evaluation Schedule for the Inspection of Maintained Schools and Academies* (2012): 12

You (and your students) must be very clear about how to progress in your subject. You could use a continuum model to show students the different levels or steps along their learning journey. From this they can work out their starting points and where they need to go. This model is described in *The Perfect Ofsted Lesson* (Beere 2010). David Didau from the Priory School in Weston-super-Mare, has had success using it to differentiate starting points in English GCSE lessons, as shown in the diagram below:

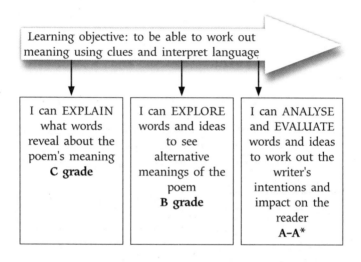

| I can EXPLAIN what words reveal about the poem's meaning **C grade** | I can EXPLORE words and ideas to see alternative meanings of the poem **B grade** | I can ANALYSE and EVALUATE words and ideas to work out the writer's intentions and impact on the reader **A–A*** |

9. Behaviour for learning

Unannounced visits for satisfactory (now predicted to be termed 'need to improve') schools are likely, particularly where behaviour has been an issue in previous inspections. All schools face the prospect of such surprise visits from September 2012, so ensuring that all teaching and discipline policies are actually consistently implemented is essential.

Above all, the leadership of the school must ensure that behaviour in the classroom and around the school is conducive to students thriving in an atmosphere of mutual respect.

The descriptor for 'outstanding' behaviour sets the bar at a high level:

> Pupils show very high levels of engagement, courtesy, collaboration and cooperation in and out of lessons. They have excellent, enthusiastic attitudes to learning, enabling lessons to proceed without interruption. Pupils are consistently punctual in arriving at school and lessons. They are highly adept at managing their own behaviour in the classroom and in social situations, supported by systematic, consistently applied approaches to behaviour management.
>
> Ofsted, *Evaluation Schedule for the Inspection of Maintained Schools and Academies* (2012): 16

Inspectors must consider:

> how well teachers manage the behaviour and expectations of pupils to ensure that all pupils have an equal and fair chance to thrive and learn in an atmosphere of respect and dignity.
>
> Ofsted, *Evaluation Schedule for the Inspection of Maintained Schools and Academies* (2012): 14

Sir Michael Wilshaw, the new head of Ofsted, has already made it very clear that he expects school leaders to use their powers to insist on zero tolerance of any behaviour that is not conducive to *all* students being able to make good progress in the classroom.

No matter how good your lesson plan or teaching is, expect any misbehaviour, lateness or off-task activity in the classroom that isn't effectively dealt with, according to school policy, to severely restrict the judgement of your teaching.

Behaviour *for* learning also includes asking good questions, challenging assumptions, contributing to community enquiry and managing time and thinking. For 'outstanding' lessons, developing the habits of great learners (see Beere 2003) will be part of every lesson.

10. Planning for success - rigorous consistency

> Teaching should be understood to include teacher's planning and implementing of learning activities across the whole curriculum as well as marking, assessment and feedback. It comprises activities within and outside the classroom, such as support and intervention.
>
> Ofsted, *Evaluation Schedule for the Inspection of Maintained Schools and Academies* (2012): 11

Planning engaging, challenging tasks that relate to the real world outside of school is the best way to ensure positive behaviour. You will also need to establish a consistent, relentless approach to a classroom ethos that has zero tolerance of any disruption of learning. Be meticulous and monomaniacal about establishing kindness, confidence and a love of learning. The habits of behaviour that you have established will be obvious to any inspector. The most powerful way to do this is to enlist the students themselves to:

- Create their own set of 'brilliant learning' laws that fit in with the school's behaviour policy but which create a 'buy in' for your particular subject and context. Display them prominently and refer to them often

- Make 'supporting learning for all' a focus for reward and praise

■ Use football and other team analogies to show how working together makes us all winners

■ Explain that they all make more progress when they support each other

■ Say often 'I'm not going to give up on you' until the reluctant learners finally give in and get on with it

(For more on this see Hook and Vass 2000.)

The most important role of teaching is to raise pupils' achievement. It is also important in promoting their spiritual, moral, social and cultural development. Teaching includes planning and implementing of learning activities across the whole curriculum, as well as marking assessment and feedback. It comprises activities within and outside the classroom, such as support and intervention.

The judgement on the quality of teaching must take account of *evidence* of pupils' learning and progress ...

Outstanding Teaching

Much of the teaching in all key stages and most subjects is outstanding and never less than consistently good. As a result, almost all pupils are making rapid and sustained progress. All teachers have consistently high expectations of all pupils. Drawing on excellent subject

---

knowledge, teachers plan astutely and set challenging tasks based on systematic, accurate assessment of pupils' prior skills, knowledge and understanding. They use well-judged and often imaginative teaching strategies that, together with sharply focused and timely support and intervention, match individual needs accurately. Consequently, pupils learn exceptionally well across the curriculum. The teaching of reading, writing, communication and mathematics is highly effective. Teachers and other adults generate high levels of enthusiasm for, participation in and commitment to learning. Teaching promotes pupils' high levels of resilience, confidence and independence when they tackle challenging activities. Teachers systematically and effectively check pupils' understanding throughout lessons, anticipating where they may need to intervene and doing so with notable impact on the quality of learning. Time is used very well and every opportunity is taken to successfully develop crucial skills, including being able to use their literacy, and numeracy skills in other subjects. Appropriate and regular homework contributes very well to pupils' learning. Marking and constructive feedback from teachers and pupils are frequent and of a consistently high quality, which leading to high levels of engagement and interest.

Ofsted, *Evaluation Schedule for the Inspection of Maintained Schools and Academies* (2012): 11–12

Top tips for an 'outstanding' focus (whether you are to be inspected or not!)

In the classroom:

- Always make *progress* your mantra – make sure the pupils know how your lesson objectives will deliver this

- Engagement – from the very start. If something exciting happens at the very beginning they are less likely to be late!

- Focus on vulnerable learners – know who they are in your school and have strategies that work

- Use of teaching assistants – use your most expensive resource to make more progress

- Behaviour for learning – non-negotiable from top down and bottom up. Use the agreed policy and nurture the habits of great learners

- Literacy in every lesson – never miss a chance to flag it up

- Questioning – more questions, open questions, especially from the students

- Responsive assessment that informs future planning – give specific, developmental feedback *and* use each assessment to help plan how to address needs

- Independent learning – plan activities that develop habitual self-management and self-confidence in learning
- Create resilience to critical feedback by modelling every mistake as a learning experience
- Ensure effective behaviour management policies are consistently applied – listen to staff concerns and constantly respond to needs

In summary:

- Empower your middle leaders so that they know exactly the quality of their team and feel accountable for it
- Use your learning champions – ASTs or your own brand of ATs – to lead your continuous improvement and deliver your coaching strategy
- Give the students a chance to feed back to add to the evaluation
- Make your peer observation programme a tool that gives you a reliable picture of provision
- Use observation to feed back to students on how to improve – this will also impact on the teacher
- Use a live 'dashboard' analytic tool to keep a close eye on all aspects of progress
- Ensure the head teacher does thirty observations a term to moderate grades

Chapter 3

Preparing for the inspection process

When will you be inspected?

This is all quite complicated so you may need to take notes! If you had 'satisfactory' or less in the last inspection you could expect Ofsted in the near future. If you got 'outstanding' last time there is an annual risk assessment process. This will start in the third year after the last inspection by examining validated results in December/January and considering whether or not there is sufficient cause for concern to trigger an inspection.

If your results have declined below floor targets or your value added looks blue on RAISEonline, especially if it is a declining trend, you will be considered for inspection. RAISEonline data will also be triangulated with any subject inspections that have taken place since your last full section 5 inspection. Any other relevant data – such as attendance figures, submissions to Parent View or any 'qualifying complaints' made by parents (under section 11A-C of the Education Act 2005) –

are also considered. If these also have any negative indications then expect an inspection imminently.

Schools judged to be 'good' in their last inspection will also be risk assessed as they approach their third year, but in any case should expect to be inspected at five year intervals. You can also pay for an inspection to take place earlier if you want to re-categorise your school. However, this is very expensive, so there is even more reason to get it right when Ofsted are scheduled to come in.

The Education Act 2011 states that, from January 2012, most schools that were judged to be outstanding at their last full section 5 inspection (including academy convertors) will be exempt from routine inspection, unless concerns are raised about their performance.

Most schools judged to be good will be inspected within five rather than three years, depending on the results of the risk assessment process.

Ofsted, *Risk Assessment of Maintained Schools and Academies* (2011): 4–5

Two days' notice – if you get it!

You have been expecting the call – and you get it. The call usually comes on either a Monday or Friday, booking you in for your date with destiny. The lead inspector will request your SEF, and other documentation relevant to questions raised, to be accessible when they arrive. The lead inspector will also be available the day before the inspection, should you need to speak to them to help make any final arrangements.

Their ideal scenario is that your SEF is brief, accurate and thorough and that by producing it you have already written the inspection report for them. The biggest complaint inspectors make about the SEF is that it is too long and too descriptive. If yours is long, trim it down so that it simply contains judgements on performance with a brief outline of the evidence base for the judgements and references to where the detailed evidence for the judgements can be found. Don't leave this until the call comes. Keep your SEF tight and succinct by editing it ruthlessly and regularly, removing descriptive detail and including evidence for judgements.

'The first contact by the lead inspector with the school is their phone call to the school to set up the inspection. The pre-inspection briefing is sent in by 4 p.m. on the day before the inspection begins though many lead inspectors will try and send it earlier in the afternoon. The phone call can be anything from half an hour to an hour long – this will depend on the complexity of the school, the background information that the lead inspector needs to know, how fast the head talks and how focused the head is in answering questions. Heads don't need to dwell on points that are not important at this stage because they can wait till the inspection happens.'

Quoted from conversations
with an Ofsted lead inspector

After the call you will then receive the pre-inspection briefing (PIB). This is a draft report that gives you an idea of what the inspection team have already gleaned from public information on results, school context, size, attendance, initial performance observations and so on. Read this very carefully and see if you agree with their commentary. The PIB is designed to raise certain questions about the school provision and performance that need to be answered. Your job is to provide accurate, succinct answers that are quick and easy to process. Less is more here. They won't have time to wade through stacks of ring binders or copious notes. (But do have evidence to hand in case they request it or if you need it to refute a judgement you think they might be making in error.)

The data

The detailed evidence (the ring binders and notes) to back up your judgements in the SEF need to be readily available in school, so make sure a copy of it is put in the room where the inspection team will be based. Be selective – they won't need all the data for everything! Focus on the questions raised in the PIB or on the evidence for judgements you have made in the SEF. Organise it in an easily accessible way. For example, if the English results have taken a dip for free school meals boys then have the action you have taken and its impact on current results, complete with specific examples, available on one sheet of A4.

You will already have your data analysed and know exactly which pupils you are targeting with which intervention. But preparing for imminent inspection means you need to sort out the relevant, clearly analysed and annotated files for these pupils from your data. You will already have produced reports for governors, staff and parents but be careful that the analysis you produce for inspectors is completely spin free. Any suspected distortion of attainment will give exactly the wrong impression. Inspectors are expert at detecting a statistical cover-up – it is always best to admit the weak spots as long as you are very clear on what is being done about them. However, raw data can be misleading and you will know the full reasons and human stories behind the outcomes for your school. Have them ready if they are not already in your SEF.

For example, Ofsted may not know why some pupils under-performed or know about those who weren't on roll but performed well and who would add to your value-added scores. Work that out for them and show them the new result – including names. Know the story behind the looked-after child and their performance in simple quantitative terms. Make sure that your middle leaders also have such examples to hand – especially in the core subjects.

The results need to be shown in relation to national stand-ards and, for the past three years, to show trends. Be ready to respond to requests for additional information by digging into your detailed evidence. There will be things you haven't thought of or extra information required about a particular group of pupils. Be prepared!

Current progress is crucial, so spreadsheets showing pupil progress since the beginning of the academic year, module test results and coursework marks are powerful indicators – especially if they exceed Fischer Family Trust data. Have this available – especially if it presents an argument for 'outstand-ing' or substantiates claims in your SEF about 'vulnerable' groups of pupils.

According to the evaluation schedule (Ofsted 2012b: 5), depending on the type of school, such vulnerable pupils may include:

■ Disabled pupils, as defined by the Equality Act 2010, and those who have special educational needs
■ Boys

- Girls
- Groups of pupils whose prior attainment may be different from that of other groups
- Those who are academically more or less able
- Pupils for whom English is an additional language
- Minority ethnic pupils
- Gypsy, Roma and Traveller children
- Looked-after children
- Pupils known to be eligible for free school meals
- Lesbian, gay and bisexual pupils
- Transgender pupils
- Young carers
- Pupils from low income backgrounds
- Other vulnerable groups

For primary schools and some secondary schools there will be a particular focus on weaker readers to check their current standard and progress in reading. Results of the most recent screening check and any follow-up undertaken by the school, with evidence of its impact so far, will be a major influence on any judgement. It is wise to have this information clearly available for inspectors to consider.

To be 'outstanding' your data must prove that:

> Almost all pupils, including where applicable, disabled pupils and those with special educational needs, are making rapid and sustained progress in most subjects over time given their starting points. They learn exceptionally well and as a result acquire knowledge quickly and in depth and are developing their understanding rapidly in a wide range of different subjects across the curriculum, including those in the sixth form and areas of learning in the Early Years Foundation Stage.
>
> Ofsted, *Evaluation Schedule for the Inspection of Maintained Schools and Academies* (2012): 9

Attainment will be expected to be at least in line with or above average national standards. If it isn't, you must be able to demonstrate that any gap for any group is closing quickly and dramatically.

The leaders – including governors

As part of your school self-evaluation process your leadership team, including governors, will have experienced subject reviews or a Mocksted (a mock inspection) and helped to write the SEF. So they will be in a strong position to know how their roles relate to the judgements on the school's performance. They will also know how to explain the vision, direction and actions the school has taken to be as good as it can be.

When inspectors talk to different groups in school, they will be looking for consistency of message, showing a common purpose and how well this triangulates with other indicators such as the data, the classroom observation and parents' feedback. This is no time for false modesty but it is appropriate to be realistic about what still needs to be done.

Identify any weak teachers in advance and explain how you are addressing their performance as part of a formal process. If you can show progress is being made, they may not include them as being typical of the teaching at your school.

Case study

Southam College is an average sized school in a market town in Warwickshire which has had 'good' inspections in the past but in 2011 got the coveted 'outstanding'.

The school has an outstanding capacity to develop further. The new head teacher is passionate about the school's development. Together with his strong team of senior leaders and with outstanding support of the governing body, he has rigorously and successfully identified and tackled areas of weakness. This has resulted in considerable improvement in many areas of the school's work since the last inspection.

Southam College, Ofsted Inspection (2011)

How does a head teacher deliver this within eighteen months of taking headship and before the data shows 'outstanding' progress on RAISEonline? Answer: clear vision, the highest expectations and relentless attention to detail. When a head walks the talk, every day, aspiration becomes contagious. However, also having a plan for the days Ofsted are in so that they get to see the impact of current actions being taken, and then being relentlessly determined to argue the case for the school's current outstanding progress, can pay dividends.

Ranjit Samra had a very clear focus when he took on the headship and he led from the front. He is out and about constantly around the school, walking the corridors, talking to students to remind them about their shirt and tie or to compliment them on something they have done – always reinforcing his vision of 'outstanding'. The day before Ofsted came I did a learning walk with Ranjit as a practice run. When we entered every room, every student was doing up their tie or tucking in their shirt – not from fear, but from unadulterated respect and affection for a head who has made every student and teacher buy in to his 'tough love' regime and relentlessly enforced high standards.

The same rigorous attention to detail was put into tracking and monitoring at the school, making it a tool to seek out underperformance, wherever it was hiding. During the inspection, Ranjit could produce the names of, and detailed reasons for, the underperformance of any student who'd had an adverse distorting impact on the overall outcomes. Each of these pupils' data was presented in a folder showing when they had come to the school and what had been done to address their needs. Each vulnerable group, as detected by the school's online data, was also identified, extensively reviewed, analysed and monitored. For example, four students had skewed the value-added data and he was able to show in detail what had happened to them and why and what had been done about it.

He was also able to show the *current* progress of Year 11 according to tracking and external exam performance. He had undertaken extensive subject reviews and restructured where he had detected performance wasn't improving. He had seconded a young, dynamic middle leader into the SLT to add an innovative fresh approach to a longstanding leadership team. Ranjit used his school improvement partner to deliver INSET and to get the teachers focused on 'progress'. All the training and CPD had one clear focus: learning. Observations were rigorous and frequent with support and return visits for those teachers who couldn't get 'good'.

The data didn't say 'outstanding' when the Ofsted team came – Ranjit told the story of the data and let the ethos around the school speak for itself. Ofsted's judgement was endorsed by the school's 2011 results when Southam

College achieved outstanding improvement in results – with 93% A*-C (and 76% A*-C, including English and maths), which represented excellent progress 'as a result of the exceptional commitment of the head teacher which directly inspires the SLT and all staff and students to buy into the ethos of raising aspiration and expectation'. Ofsted added that: 'Sophisticated tracking of student progress enables leaders to identify and address underachievement and to set challenging targets.'

The staff, students, parents and governors

Staff

As soon as you know about an inspection tell the staff immediately so that they can prepare their very best lessons. The head presenting the inspection as an opportunity rather than a threat is probably the most important aspect of staff preparation. Empowering staff to want to show off and be observed because the school is delivering an excellent education will spread a contagious confidence and can-do atmosphere. Get the staff to skim read *The Perfect Ofsted Lesson* (Beere 2010) if they want to remind themselves that lessons are all about learning and the progress the students are making – not about them. What staff do five hours a day, five days a week ultimately impacts on the outcomes for the school.

Reassure staff that a detailed lesson plan isn't as important as being able to give inspectors information about the ability and make-up of the class and the learning objective for the lesson. Detailed lesson plans are time consuming to make and probably won't be read in full, but any observer will want to know how the teacher intends to make progress and what the needs of the class are.

Additional tips to help staff get through classroom observation may also be useful. For example, use a mini-plenary when an inspector walks into the room to let them know what is going on and show the progress made so far. Always try to enable the pupils to demonstrate the progress made. A teacher-led plenary would only be 'satisfactory'. A 'good' lesson would have progress demonstrated through pupils discussing work with each other and then sharing outcomes with the teacher. An 'outstanding' lesson would involve the pupils themselves demonstrating the progress in learning, recording it themselves and being able to apply it to a new context. If staff are nervous, it helps to get the pupils up to the front and showing off what great learners they are – always impressive!

Marking should, of course, be up to date and be focused on target setting – no bland comments or pages of ticks.

The classrooms should look cared for, respected and good for learning – but these things cannot be done in a day. Hopefully, the culture and habits developed before an inspection will already be delivering all that is required for the perfect lesson.

In classrooms with vulnerable pupils, the part that teaching assistants play in lessons can really influence the judgements made. Make sure TAs feel included and know that their job is to make an impact on the learning and progress of the pupils they work with – not to babysit or do the work for them. I'm sure they won't need reminding of this in your school; it is what they do (see page 66 for more on the use of TAs).

Checklist for staff

- ▨ Be prompt to the lesson and prompt to start the learning
- ▨ Set engaging objectives and ensure you can demonstrate *progress* in learning
- ▨ Make sure all the pupils' books are available
- ▨ Plan your lessons to enable a mini-plenary when an inspector calls in
- ▨ Ensure you have opportunities for active learning
- ▨ Use students to teach each other and present their own learning
- ▨ Keep up a good pace but include some reflection and improvement time
- ▨ Show how you use assessment to inform future learning
- ▨ Address *any* misbehaviour by using the school behaviour policy
- ▨ Relax and enjoy your lesson – it's an opportunity to show off

Remember: it's not about you; it's about *their* learning. And keep in mind that the rest of the year is even more important than the inspection!

Students

The students will want to be part of the whole experience as they want to feel 'outstanding' too. Telling them that they can talk to the inspectors openly at the right moments and show off their work and books is demonstrating your trust and faith in them. Conversations with pupils can show so much about the school, including how confident they are speaking to strangers and, hopefully, that they are aware of the school's strengths and challenges. Pupils also love to be in the group that volunteer to talk to inspectors or show them around the school.

The kinds of questions inspectors always ask in classrooms are: 'Why are you doing that?', 'How does that help you learn?' and 'What do you need to do next to make progress?' If you have followed the guidance in previous chapters then students will be used to such questions. They will have a language for learning that helps them reflect on what strategies they use when they are stuck and how group work helps them learn. Unfortunately, more than one school has had their inspection undermined by a small group of students who wanted to cause mischief and mislead inspectors. The answer is to involve such ringleaders who clearly have leadership potential. You know who they are – and if you don't then you don't deserve 'outstanding'! So low-key assemblies informing the pupils about what is happening and their role in it should be routine; involving as many of them as possible in showing off your school is essential.

Parents

It is important to welcome into school those parents who may have had an axe to grind. You will know who they are as you have managed your own Parent View forum as suggested in Chapter 1. Make them feel involved in the inspection and give them a voice. You have already responded to their concerns respectfully and thoroughly, with all parties feeling they have been heard. Have brief evidence of this, such as meetings held, including dates and parents' signatures, in the room where you accommodate the inspectors.

Governors

Make sure your chair of governors has been involved in writing and reviewing your school SEF so that they are clear about the strengths and weaknesses of the school and how they have supported and challenged your action plan. It is beneficial to have available a governor who has been monitoring any vulnerable aspects, such as boys' literacy or more-able pupils, to show the impact of action taken.

The environment

Ensuring the school looks as good as it can is common sense. When you sell your home the smell of baking bread is said to create the feel-good factor. When you are selling your school be aware that how our senses respond to our environment can have a powerful impact on judgements. If it looks, sounds and smells nice it will help. However, if your school looks, sounds and smells nice all year round, that is even better. There is no head or member of the SLT who doesn't pick up litter at some time during the day, so make sure you don't have to do that on inspection day by having a regular system of litter picks by pupils.

Classrooms and corridors will need to be refreshed, tidied and checked for new graffiti. But if they looked lived in, this is to be expected in a busy school. At this stage, teachers should be busy planning great lessons, not hiding away sloppy piles of unmarked books.

Making the inspector's job easier

Ensure that you send the inspection team a map and a local accommodation list in plenty of time, as they may be travelling from afar and will be working flat out to prepare for your inspection. In the couple of days before an inspection, don't forget to arrange parking spaces, send detailed directions and organise a warm, quiet, welcoming room for the inspection team to work in. This room needs to be near the front of the school so that they don't have to fight their way past pupils in the canteen, through the bike sheds or across the playground out to a distant mobile every time they need to reflect on how good the school is!

Make available all the paperwork they require in a simple, easy-to-access format, labelled and summarised to answer any questions that might emerge from the inspection process. Include a copy of your 'safer recruitment' staff central records and have a school timetable pinned up on the wall alongside your vision statement and action plan priorities. Access to the internet and the school's intranet may also be useful for quick reference. Have plenty of coffee, tea and biscuits and sandwiches supplied to them by helpful pupils whenever required. The team will be under real time pressure, so think of how you can make it as easy and comfortable for them as possible. Offer them the 'outstanding' hospitability that is part of the 'way you do things'. They are only human and will appreciate your efforts.

On the day, make sure that reception is open and staffed very early with an efficient, welcoming receptionist fully briefed on the correct 'safe' procedure for visitors.

What not to do!

Rising numbers of schools are resorting to underhand tactics to give a favourable impression of classroom standards.

Daily Telegraph, 6 January 2012

According to this article, the following tactics are apparently what some schools have used to try and improve their inspection outcome:

- Arranged for a last-minute trip to Alton Towers for the most challenging students
- Advised the worst teacher to go off sick
- Got pupils to rehearse their best lessons and perform them for inspectors
- Bought in an AST from the local 'outstanding' school to place with their worst class
- Paid teachers extra to deliver fantastic lessons just for Ofsted
- Bought new furniture that you have sworn you can't afford for three years
- Bribed certain students to stay at home
- Borrowed good display work from a nearby school and put it up on their walls
- Got in a supply teacher to babysit the students that misbehave

Alternatively, you can follow the advice in this book!

Top tips for the days before

- Make sure you get a clear idea of what Ofsted are thinking in the first planning phone call with the lead inspector. During this make a to-do list to work your way through in the next two days

- Respond to the PIB by providing succinct information that answers the questions
- Send a map and helpful details about parking and accommodation
- Prepare a comfortable private room with access to refreshments and any vital information
- Ensure reception staff are fully briefed about appropriate procedures
- Inform staff and give them a simple checklist (see page 117 for a for photocopiable checklist)
- Inform students and assign some of them to helpful roles
- Ensure your data is clearly analysed, with reference to any weak spots identified and action taken
- Brief your middle managers about their role in joint observation
- Do a learning walk across the whole school with an objective observer (your school improvement partner maybe) to see the school as Ofsted will see it. Plan the inspectors' initial walk of the school to ensure they see the best bits first
- Go to the gym or for a brisk walk. Eat and sleep well
- Visualise a great inspection!

Chapter 4

On the day

STOP PRESS! Proposed 'no notice' inspections from September 2012 mean that you should have a wonderful welcome routine available for any visitors that visit the school unexpectedly. You may not be able to make it all happen quite like this, but consider the following with 'no notice' in mind.

The welcome

The inspection team will arrive early and the number of inspectors will depend on the size of the school. Their parking places will be reserved and the room the team will be based in is ready. Remember, first impressions count. The primacy effect means that our perception is massively influenced by the first smells, sights and sounds and the feelings they generate.

Make all the appropriate checks and introductions during the signing-in process and then arrange for refreshments to be delivered to the room by a (cheerful) child assigned with taking catering orders for the day. It's good to let the inspection team meet children immediately and in as many informal situations as possible, because they represent what the school is all about.

The first school walk

After the first meeting the inspector will want to walk around and get a feel for the school with the head. Ensure that this walk shows your school at its very best. Moving around the school with the Ofsted team leader is the moment of truth when you will (hopefully) feel that immense sense of pride in your school as you see it at work through the eyes of a professional inspector. Nothing should surprise you if you have done this walk before very recently. You will have prepared the route to call in at classrooms where the teacher is expecting you and you are confident a great first impression will be given. Already a view is forming in the mind of the inspector because your interaction with teachers and children as well as your running commentary is now forming part of your school's story.

The pupils for the focus groups will meet with the inspection team during their visit. In the new inspection framework, inspectors are expected to decide who will take part in those groups. The school needs to have lists available of different groups of children alongside current levels and targets from which the inspection team can choose a wide range of ages and abilities.

Telling your story

The way you and others tell the story of your school will set the context for judgements. Be honest, open and optimistic. You know the context and history of your school and you need to reiterate this in a positive, powerful way without being defensive about the weak spots or over-exaggerating the accomplishments. Be honest about what else needs to be done and *how* you are tackling it. Be proud of your achievements and emphasise them. How you present the story of your school is crucial to the development of the impression the inspector will have of you and your provision for the pupils. This is true of all the leadership team and the staff. What story will they tell about your school? Is it the same as yours? Will the children tell the same story? Inspection is a triangulation of many different judgements, and the story frames the bigger picture of the judgements.

Prepare a folder that responds specifically to all the points raised in the first conversation and the PIB. Include in this specific evidence of why you are 'good' or 'outstanding' (or whatever your SEF has judged you as). Include current progress evidence, such as recent results, relevant pages from RAISEonline that highlight performance of certain groups, sections of the SDP/SEF relevant to questions raised, recent governors' reports and logs of work on mentoring certain vulnerable children. Know the names of every pupil attached to every spot on the value-added graph who underperformed and why they did. All of this will be available elsewhere but it is vital that you can quickly and efficiently put your hands on the key information and tell the story behind it.

There is nothing worse than being asked a question about your school and not knowing the answer. However, during an inspection this is bound to happen sometimes – to the head or anyone else who is interviewed. The main thing is to be able to find the evidence quickly and, if it isn't available, to be honest and learn from it.

Have a list of which teachers may be observed on the first day that relate to questions from the PIB and be ready to discuss strengths and challenges in the teaching staff. The inspection team will first of all want to know if your judgements of the teaching and learning in your school are accurate. This will mean checking out whether they agree with your records. Have your spreadsheet of all the observations completed over the year to hand, all RAG rated to show who has had extra support and coaching and for what. This is evidence that you have an excellent tracking system for assessing teacher performance; alongside it have all your performance management information to show action taken when teachers needed to improve. After the first day the team will be more confident that your judgements on teaching and learning are correct and, if this triangulates with the data about outcomes, you are heading towards a positive judgement on leadership. Then they will want to look for more evidence to substantiate the judgement so may ask to see specific subjects or teachers.

Involving parents in the inspection process is very helpful – sometimes these can include members of staff. Inspectors will already have some parental feedback but having parents in school to talk about how issues are dealt with can be helpful. It is better if the parents have had children through the school and so can offer a view on how homework has changed in recent years or how the school communicates about careers. Parental engagement is a focus in the new framework, so examples of how reluctant parents have been involved in the school will be important – especially if the context demonstrates an achievement gap for children from under-privileged families.

Top tips

Christopher Whitehead Language College, a large secondary school near Worcester, achieved 'outstanding' in their inspection in June 2010. Head teacher Neil Morris gives his five top suggestions on how to prepare for Ofsted.

■ **Train as a whole staff:** Far too often head teachers are persuaded by middle managers to 'split' valuable days into department time/preparation time and do not gather together their staff to ensure a collective message is followed. We had excellent professional trainers which I would recommend especially for a September 'kick start' to a year. These trainers challenge your school, your department, your staff and you. They make you ask what kind of school you would like to be and what you expect your staff to achieve. Professional training is required; not the humdrum start to the year that can happen – full of administration, lists and notices that make staff perspire rather than inspire them to make a major difference.

Know the criteria: Expect your teaching staff to be observed and ensure or engineer good observation whether it be peer observation or 'drop-ins'. Know what a good lesson looks like. Make observations part of the school review system. To ensure this is not threatening take away the judgement scores and make staff look at the comments, not the 1–4 grading that can minimise meaningful feedback.

Involve the whole community in your journey: Getting all parents and students involved is essential and makes them feel pride in their school. There are invaluable, anonymous annual surveys available that take account of their views and can be published/ recorded. Then you just need to reflect on the results and act on them.

Decide on your unique selling point: This should be something that you will not budge on, no matter what the budget cuts or the latest government whim. We are an effective language college in a predominantly white British community with growing social unrest. The school has a vertical tutor system, which is part of a proactive house system which gave us a clear identity and was something we felt staff, students and parents had 'bought into'.

■ **Decide where you are going to base the Ofsted team and understand their requirements:** I wanted to have a member of the leadership team who was Ofsted trained. We hadn't got around to it but it still remains a desirable aim that ensures a member of your team can understand the criteria and their requirements. Ofsted work hard and understanding what they require is essential. We gave them a quiet office with key information and evidence of our own evaluations of impact. We did our preparation and knew the grades for each area of the inspection and which grades were limiting.

Partnership with the inspection team

Inspections are now conducted in partnership with the school leaders. The team will welcome joint observations with senior and middle leaders and will often ask what their judgement is before explaining their own. This will result in a professional conversation about the learning. It is important that your middle leaders are confident enough to challenge judgements – especially when they are working with non-specialist inspectors. This means making sure that notes taken during lessons are detailed and contain real examples of evidence to support judgements so that professional arguments can be made when necessary.

In addition, the head and SLT will be present during inspectors' discussions about various judgements so there are opportunities to listen and present further evidence and to challenge points that you feel are wrong assumptions. Many schools have found the team are open to being persuaded by additional evidence because they are well aware that in two days they may miss important aspects that are highly relevant. It is up to the school to ensure that nothing good is missed and that no judgement is made without it being fair and justified. Be relentless in arguing your case with the team, but only if you can produce clear evidence to prove you are right. The outcome is not a summary of all the lesson observation judgements but an overall judgement of school provision across all the indicators, so inevitably there is a measure of subjectivity. However, inspectors must show evidence for their decisions, so if you disagree you will also need clear evidence.

Your chair of governors can be a great asset if present and involved in the inspection. They have to demonstrate good leadership and it is a very useful exercise for them to be able to contribute and hear the feedback first hand. If they can also contribute with examples and evidence of action taken to address issues that involved governors, all the better.

If a crisis occurs during the two days – which it probably will – prioritise sorting it out in the same way that you would normally. You still have a school to run and the team know this. Your response to events will be noted, so respond just as your 'vision' dictates.

Afterwards

The inspection process is often draining and exhausting for everyone but if you feel the draft report is fair then it may all be worthwhile. Feedback collected by Ofsted suggests that the benefits outweigh the negatives. This is the view of the large majority of schools who respond to the Ofsted consultation process. The more positively you have approached the process, the more you will gain from it.

Action points will be highlighted in the report and no matter what the outcome you will want to draft an action plan in response to it. This is particularly true if you get the coveted 'outstanding' judgement because there is some evidence that the metaphoric 'sigh of relief' in the year after such an inspection can lead to a decline in outcomes. So it is important to quickly decide, in consultation with staff and students, what the next stage of development beyond 'outstanding' will be. My option is always to go for 'world class'!

There will be some staff who feel cheated because they didn't get observed or because their grade was disappointing. They may not feel part of the outcome, so it is important that the debrief given for everyone makes a clear focus on the team effort that has delivered the long-term culture and outcomes that resulted in the judgement report. This includes support and administrative staff who are often also parents and members of the local community.

The inspection outcome – whatever that is – can be the most important lever for a school to move forward. It gives an opportunity to take radical action to address the need for improvement. The inspection aims to offer advice for addressing the needs of the school, so detailed long-term post-inspection action planning should involve everybody.

What if it is unexpectedly bad? Self-evaluation will need to be addressed and maybe time set aside to move some staff forward or out of teaching. For some schools this is the beginning of a process of self-awareness and improvement that they can look back on and see as the catalyst for change. Reread this book, create a shared action plan and know the only way is up!

What if it was bad but expected? Then you have the capacity to know what you need to do to move forward and put it right. Now you have the strategies and feedback to galvanise your staff and governors to take those difficult decisions – because the inspectors will be back and the scrutiny will only increase until things start to improve.

What if it delivers the 'perfect' outcome? The party you hold to celebrate the end of the inspection will no doubt be remembered by all. But, whatever the judgement, the provision for your pupils over the long term, day in, day out, is still the reward that will make the most difference.

Respect, love and learning, embedded and celebrated for all the school years, will provide the legacy for happy and successful future citizens that lasts far longer than Ofsted. Keeping all of that in proportion when the Ofsted report is such high stakes can be very hard. Getting a great report requires excellent preparation and long-term planning but also a degree of luck. Some schools plaster 'outstanding' all over their paperwork, reception and buildings, if they are lucky enough to achieve it; some just keep building their legacy and know that once it's over – it's just the beginning.

2012 Ofsted framework summary

Overall effectiveness – how good is the school?

Four areas to judge: *Achievement, Behaviour, Quality of teaching,* and *Leadership and Management* plus spiritual, moral, social and cultural

Achievement judged by:

- How the gaps are narrowing between different groups of pupils
- Teaching must engage, enthuse and motivate pupils so they learn and make progress
- Standards achieved by the time they leave the school compared to national average – trends in school results
- Pupil progress relative to starting points
- Quality of work and progress over time
- Progress of disabled and special educational needs (SEN) pupils
- Standards and progress in literacy/oracy

Behaviour judged by:

- Conduct in lessons and around school
- Behaviour, respect and attitudes of pupils and adults
- Views of parents and pupils
- Safety from bullying and harassment
- Attendance and punctuality at school and in lessons

Quality of teaching judged by:

- Assessment of pupils' progress
- Planning learning to enhance all pupils' progress
- Providing constructive feedback to deliver progress over time

Teachers must:

- Demonstrate high expectation
- Set challenging tasks
- Use expertise to deepen knowledge and understanding
- Teach pupils the skills they need to learn for themselves
- Plan the lesson to meet the needs of all pupils
- Ensure that teaching and support stretches each individual pupil, including disabled and SEN
- Effectively teach children to read and develop literacy skills

Leadership judged by how head and leaders:

- Provide an appropriate curriculum that helps all children achieve well
- Improve the school and show capacity for sustaining improvement
- Show ambition for pupils and improvements in pupil achievement, teaching and learning
- Support and develop staff
- Ensure the accuracy of school self-evaluation and use made of findings
- Improve teaching and learning
- Promote confidence and engagement of parents
- Work in partnership with other schools and external agencies to improve further
- Ensure equality of opportunity
- Effectively safeguard pupils

Plus:

- The impact of governance on school improvement

Quick checklist for staff

1. Be prompt to the lesson and prompt to start the learning ☑
2. Set engaging objectives and ensure you can demonstrate *progress* in learning ☑
3. Make sure all the pupils' books are available ☑
4. Plan your lessons to enable a mini-plenary when an inspector calls in ☑
5. Ensure you have opportunities for active learning ☑
6. Use students to teach each other and present their own learning ☑
7. Keep up a good pace but include some reflection and improvement time ☑
8. Show how you use assessment to inform future learning ☑
9. Address *any* misbehaviour by using the school behaviour policy ☑
10. Relax and enjoy your lesson – it's an opportunity to show off ☑

Good luck!

Final checklist for inspection

Have you:

1. Ensured you have to hand all the essential PIB answers with evidence to hand in a folder ☑

2. Prepared a delightful welcome and work-base near the front of the school with everything they need in close proximity ☑

3. Involved some helpful children from the start ☑

4. Planned a wonderful tour of the school to create a good first impression ☑

5. Planned to guide the team to lessons that can demonstrate your school's accurate judgements on teaching and learning ☑

6. Ensured you encourage middle leaders to observe with the inspection team and to collect good evidence of their judgements ☑

7. Prepared to be involved yourself in the debates and discussions and provide extra evidence when required ☑

Good luck!

And afterwards

1. Support staff who may be upset by the process ☑
2. Set up a new plan of action based on issues raised ☑
3. Remember that ultimately it's the day-to-day life of your school that really matters ☑

References and further reading

Beere, J. (2003). *The Learner's Toolkit*. Crown House Publishing.

Beere, J. (2010). *The Perfect Ofsted Lesson*. Crown House Publishing.

Duckworth, J. (2009). *The Little Book of Values*. Crown House Publishing.

Dweck, C. S. (2007). *Mindset: The New Psychology of Success*. Ballantine.

Gilbert, I. (2002). *Essential Motivation in the Classroom*. Routledge Farmer.

Ginnis, P. (2002). *The Teacher's Toolkit: Raise Classroom Achievement with Activities for Every Learner*. Crown House Publishing.

Goleman, D. (1996). *Emotional Intelligence: Why It Can Matter More Than IQ*. Bloomsbury.

Hattie, J. (2012). *Visible Learning for Teachers: Maximizing Impact on Learning*. Routledge.

Higgins, S., Kokotsaki, D. and Coe, R. (2011). *Toolkit of Strategies to Improve Learning: Summary for Schools Spending the Pupil Premium*. Sutton Trust and the Centre for Evaluation and Monitoring, Durham University. Available at http://www.suttontrust.com/public/documents/toolkit-summary-final-r-2-.pdf (accessed 24 January 2012).

Hook, P. and Vass, A. (2000). *Confident Classroom Leadership*. David Fulton Publishers.

Kayembe, G. (2008). *Engaging Parents as Stakeholders*. Tribal.

Ofsted (2011a). *Inspection 2012: Proposals for Inspection Arrangements for Maintained Schools and Academies from January 2012*. Ref: 110025. Available at http://www.ofsted.gov.uk/resources/inspection-2012-proposals-for-inspection-arrangements-for-maintained-schools-and-academies-january-2 (accessed 24 January 2012).

Ofsted (2011b). *Risk Assessment of Maintained Schools and Academies*. Ref. 110153. Available at http://www.ofsted.gov.uk/resources/risk-assessment-of-maintained-schools-and-academies (accessed 24 January 2012).

Ofsted (2011c). 'A New Voice for Parents'. Press release, 20 October 2011. Available at http://www.ofsted.gov.uk/news/new-voice-for-parents?news=17429 (accessed 24 January 2012).

Ofsted (2012a). *The Framework for School Inspection from January 2012*. Ref. 090019. Available at http://www.ofsted.gov.uk/

resources/framework-for-school-inspection-january-2012 (accessed 24 January 2012).

Ofsted (2012b). *The Evaluation Schedule for the Inspection of Maintained Schools and Academies from January 2012*. Ref. 090098. Available at http://www.ofsted.gov.uk/resources/ evaluation-schedule-for-inspection-of-maintained-schools-and-academies-january-2012 (accessed 24 January 2012).

Ofsted (2012c). *Subsidiary Guidance Supporting the Inspection of Maintained Schools and Academies from January 2012*. Ref. 110166. Available at http://www.ofsted.gov.uk/resources/sub-sidiary-guidance-supporting-inspection-of-maintained-schools-and-academies-january-2012 (accessed 24 January 2012).

Paton, G. (2012). 'Schools "Bribing Pupils" to Cheat Ofsted Inspections'. *Daily Telegraph*, 6 January. Available at http:// www.telegraph.co.uk/education/educationnews/8995377/ Schools-bribing-pupils-to-cheat-Ofsted-inspections.html (accessed 24 January 2012).

Ryan, W. (2011). *Inspirational Teachers, Inspirational Learners*. Crown House Publishing.

Seligman, M. (2011). *Flourish: A New Understanding of Happiness and Well-Being – and How To Achieve Them*. Nicholas Brealey.

More Jackie Beere Books ...

The Perfect Ofsted Lesson by Jackie Beere
edited by Ian Gilbert ISBN 978-1-84590-460-9

The Perfect English Lesson by David Didau
edited by Jackie Beere ISBN 978-1-78135-052-2

The Perfect Teacher Coach by Terri Broughton
and Will Thomas edited by Jackie Beere
ISBN 978-1-78135-003-4

Perfect Assessment for Learning by Claire Gadsby
edited by Jackie Beere ISBN 978-1-78135-002-7

The Primary Learner's Toolkit by Jackie Beere
edited by Ian Gilbert ISBN 978-1-84590-395-4

The Learner's Toolkit by Jackie Beere edited by Ian Gilbert
ISBN 978-1-84590-070-0

The Competency Curriculum Toolkit by Jackie Beere
and Helen Boyle ISBN 978-1-84590-126-4

 Bringing together some of the most innovative practitioners working
in education today under the guidance of Ian Gilbert, founder of
Independent Thinking Ltd. www.independentthinkingpress.com